YORK NOTES

Bleak House

Charles Dickens

Note by Richard Gravil

 Longman   York Press

YORK PRESS
322 Old Brompton Road, London SW5 9JH

PEARSON EDUCATION LIMITED
Edinburgh Gate, Harlow,
Essex CM20 2JE, United Kingdom
Associated companies, branches and representatives throughout the world

First published 2001

ISBN 0-582-42464-X

Designed by Vicki Pacey
Phototypeset by Gem Graphics, Trenance, Mawgan Porth, Cornwall
Colour reproduction and film output by Spectrum Colour
Produced by Addison Wesley Longman China Limited, Hong Kong

CONTENTS

PART ONE

INTRODUCTION

HOW TO STUDY A NOVEL

- You will need to read the novel more than once. Start by reading it quickly for pleasure, then read it slowly and thoroughly. On your second reading make detailed notes on the plot, characters, and **themes**.
- Note passages which capture each character as seen by the narrators, and their most characteristic ways of speaking. Are all characters equally rounded, or are some flat and stereotyped? Do they change?
- Is the author's personal attitude to the characters made clear? If so, is this through direct comment, plot implications (who gets killed off) or the endorsement of other characters?
- Would you say the novel has one plot or multiple plots? If the latter, are they thematically integrated?
- Think about how the novel is narrated, and about the difference between the two narratives, especially their values, their way of seeing characters and their style of narration.
- What part do settings, rural and urban, and especially the elaborate descriptions of some of the houses, play? Is the author concerned with historical accuracy?
- Are particular **images** or **symbols** repeated, and do these repetitions help you to understand the novel's themes?
- What is the effect of the novel's two endings? Do they create two different impressions, or coalesce into one overall impression?
- Is the prevailing effect that of **realism**, fable, romance, **satire**, or **allegory**?
- Does either narrative in the novel present a moral and just world? Does the novel have a didactic purpose and, if so, what is it?
- What nineteenth-century assumptions (about class, gender, religion) does the author accept or criticise?

Always cite exact sources for all quotations, from the novel and from critical commentaries, and find your own textual examples to back up your opinions.

George Bernard Shaw said of Dickens's *Hard Times*, 'This is Karl Marx, Carlyle, Ruskin, Morris, Carpenter, rising up against civilization itself as a disease'. Dickens's message, Shaw said, was that 'it is not our disorder, but our order that is horrible'. That judgement may be still more applicable to *Bleak House*, a novel in which Dickens develops a range of characters, whose manner and behaviour are close to cannibalism, to exhibit his views of capitalism. The figures mentioned by Shaw are all varieties of socialist: in fact, Dickens is no more obviously socialist than other novelists of the day, but at the time he was writing *Bleak House* he was also serialising in *Household Words* his immensely readable *A Child's History of England* which shows him to be very partisan towards Cromwell, and overtly republican.

Bleak House is one of Dickens's greatest achievements. It is rivalled only by *Great Expectations* as an experimental narrative, and by *Our Mutual Friend* for its combination of exuberant style and characterisation, with powerful **symbolic** statements diagnostic of the condition of England. On a larger scale than other 'condition of England' novels, *Bleak House* can also seem more radical. This is not because Dickens sets out any practical schemes of reform, but because he describes a social order which is clearly in terminal decay and beyond reform. England, in *Bleak House*, is suffering from some deep systemic disorder, for which the only cure, it seems, might be purgation by fire. Although you may not notice this on a first reading (you will be too busy trying to follow the plot and remember who is who) one of the recurring motifs of the novel is a tendency for things to collapse or combust. Symbolic fires (of apocalyptic cleansing?) break out from time to time, lameness is endemic, London is reverting to mud. In one nightmarish scene, wandering through the streets of London, in search of one of its innumerable destitutes, the mild Mr Snagsby and the mysterious Mr Bucket find themselves surrounded by shadowy figures of despair, reaching out from the abyss.

Bleak House is also one of the most experimental of nineteenth-century classics. Like other famous multiple narratives, Emily Brontë's *Wuthering Heights*, and Wilkie Collins's *The Moonstone*, this novel invites the reader to become engaged in a process of judgement, while rendering that process more difficult by the very manner in which it is told. It interleaves two deeply contrasting narratives, of similar length, each with its own style, its own experience and its own values. Charles Dickens, internationally famous writer, campaigner for all kinds of reform, raconteur, wit, and man of the world, tells one half of the novel in heightened but unmistakably 'Dickensian' style. But he elects to have the other half narrated by a diffident, illegitimate young woman, a decision critics have been trying to come to terms with ever since. At times the two narrators seem to be telling quite different stories, though in fact numerous characters appear in both narratives. Our ability to follow Esther Summerson's story of her 'progress', from illegitimate childhood to happy and respectable marriage, depends crucially upon the impersonal narrator's story, which concerns the downfall of the haughty Lady Dedlock, and the disgrace she brings upon an ancient house. When you *re*-read this novel – and much of the detail of this huge book is there to be relished on a second or third reading – you will find that its structure enables you to concentrate on one narrative or the other. In all probability you will choose the impersonal narrative for your second reading, because it is remembered as funnier; and the personal narrative for your third reading, because it is in fact just as funny, but in a more humane spirit. But there is more to this 'split narrative' than technique. *Bleak House* was published at a time of unprecedented agitation on 'the woman question' and Dickens's dual narrative, shared with an illegitimate young woman who symbolises woman's exclusion from legal existence, is a major imaginative response to that major nineteenth-century issue. Although this facet of the novel has been ignored until very recently, thanks to Dickens's reputation for not understanding women, Esther's half of the book may deserve to be recognised as a minor classic of liberal feminism.

Of all the great novelists of world literature, Dickens is the one whose work has the sharpest flavour of topicality. Three of the novel's major themes, the inefficiency of the Court of Chancery, the state of sanitation in the city (and the consequent prevalence of killer diseases, such as cholera, typhus, smallpox), and the paralysis of government, were topics of the day. A fourth theme is the muddleheadedness of organised charity. Through one of his most memorable characters, Mrs Pardiggle, Dickens shows the middle class to be incapable of communicating with the working poor. In another, Mrs Jellyby, he **satirises** the folly and hypocrisy of engaging in remote and impracticable charitable activities – seeking to export civilisation from a benighted and 'boastful island'. At moments Dickens uses his immense authority as (probably) the most popular novelist of all time to appeal directly to the nation's rulers, including at one point Queen Victoria herself. And he does so, most dramatically, when dealing with the obscure death of the most insignificant of her subjects, Jo, an illiterate crossing-sweeper, dying of cholera contracted in the squalid heart of London.

Apart from these large topical issues, the novel's themes include respectability, hypocrisy, illegitimacy, duplicity, rapaciousness, exploitation, vocation, dandyism, aristocracy. To treat these themes, Dickens uses an astonishing range of associated images – fog, mud, mist, ink, sheep, skin, grease, parchment, documents, detritus, disease, pox, waste, death, decay, corruption, dust, rust, fire and brimstone. These images recur compulsively and are blent together in symbolic clusters suggestive either of entropy (the world running down) or of apocalypse (the world blowing up).

Edgar Johnson called *Bleak House*, rightly, 'this dark storm of a story'. Yet it is also brilliantly comic, an effervescent performance, and shot through with a surprising variety of reassuringly good characters. Partly because it was written for serialisation, the novel is full of realised scenes and a gallery of sharply drawn characters all with their own unique and memorable speech signatures: no two characters, in a novel with dozens, sound quite alike, even when they are intended to remind one of each other. Dickens wrote *Bleak House* in less time than it may take to study it. Yet despite the speed of its composition, *Bleak House* has touches of quite astonishing subtlety and sentences to die for.

If this sounds over the top, some critics think *Bleak House* not only Dickens's best novel, but the finest novel created in England in an age devoted to the novel. Its only serious rival for that title, apart from *Our Mutual Friend*, which you should read next, is George Eliot's *Middlemarch*. Every copy should carry a warning: 'reading Dickens may seriously damage your taste for modern fiction'. After all, there is more invention in the average Dickens *chapter* than in many prize-winning novels, and Dickens at this date was at his most inventive. Enjoy it!

PART TWO

SUMMARIES & COMMENTARIES

Bleak House *was first published in serial form, between March 1852 and September 1853, then republished in book form in 1853, on the basis of corrected proofs of the monthly parts. The page numbers in this York Note refer to* Bleak House, *ed. Nicola Bradbury (Penguin Classics, 1996). This edition follows the 1853 text, and its table of contents reproduces the serial form of publication. The chapters are clustered by monthly instalments (a Roman numeral beside the chapter number tells you when you are starting a new episode, and an appendix includes Dickens's working notes for the monthly parts). If you are using the 1971 Penguin (edited by Norman Page, with an introduction by J. Hillis Miller), the excellent introduction will amply compensate for the annoyance of having different page numbers. Because the 1996 Penguin is exhaustively annotated, this York Note deals with only the most significant terms and allusions, and with matters not noted in the text.*

SYNOPSIS

According to the reviewer in the *Illustrated London News* (24 September 1853) 'no man … could tell a story better, if he had but a story to tell': and it is true that anyone reading *Bleak House* for the plot will find it both bewildering and disappointing. Whether it really has a plot, or whether it matters, is very debatable. But it does tell three simultaneous major stories, interspersed with several minor ones. The first is that of the resolution of a long-standing case in the Court of Chancery, known as 'Jarndyce and Jarndyce', into which several generations have been born, and on which several generations of lawyers have 'fleshed' their legal wit. The living suitors in the case, which has to do with a disputed will, include John Jarndyce, a man of infinite benevolence and infinite contempt for the law and all its doings, and Richard Carstone, his ward. Richard is obsessed by the vain expectation that the case will make him rich, and he allows this expectation to divide him from John Jarndyce, who warns him repeatedly that no good ever came from a Chancery suit, except for the lawyers. (As the narrator explains, the great principle of English law is to make business for itself.) Richard's gullibility leads to his exploitation by the parasitical Harold Skimpole and a predatory lawyer, Vholes. The lure of Chancery, its spell, makes it impossible for him to settle to a sensible career. He is ruined, in health as well as financially. Secretly, he marries his fellow ward, Ada Clare, against the advice of their guardian, John Jarndyce. On his death he leaves his young wife pregnant and destitute.

The second story (connected very loosely to the first by the fact that papers relating to the two stories are eventually found in the same place) concerns the downfall of Lady Dedlock, who long before her marriage to the baronet Sir Leicester Dedlock, had a romance with Captain Hawdon. The romance produced an illegitimate child, whom she supposed to be stillborn, but who was in fact spirited away to be brought up in secret by Lady Dedlock's sister, Miss Barbary. In consultation with her lawyer, Mr Tulkinghorn, at the start of the novel, Lady Dedlock recognises the handwriting of her former lover. Mr Tulkinghorn, suspicious of her sudden interest, spends the remainder of his life, until the night of his murder, on the track of her guilty secret. Fear that she may be suspected of the murder, and either blackmailed or exposed as a fallen woman, leads to Lady Dedlock's flight and her death.

The third story is that of Lady Dedlock's illegitimate child, Esther Summerson, who narrates almost half of the chapters, and over half of the novel. Her story focuses, for the most part, on the benevolence of Mr Jarndyce, to whom she becomes engaged, and the passage of Richard and Ada from youth, hope and innocence, to romance and ruin. Reluctantly, however, and with great embarrassment, she also tells of a developing love between herself and Doctor Woodcourt, a handsome young doctor, whose useful profession symbolises that he is the romantic hero of the novel. Reluctantly, also, and without seeking it, she acquires knowledge of her parentage. This knowledge confirms (as she sees it, and as she has been told from childhood) that she is her mother's disgrace.

Connecting these three narratives, in a novel much concerned with documents and writing, is the handwriting of Esther's father. Employed as an anonymous law-writer, under the pseudonym Nemo (meaning no-one), the former Captain Hawdon has copied the document that alerts Tulkinghorn to Lady Dedlock's secret in Chapter 2, and (quite possibly) the letter Esther receives from the law firm of Kenge and Carboy in Chapter 3. In Chapter 4, Esther stands for a moment, without knowing it, outside her dying father's room. The death of Nemo frustrates Tulkinghorn's search for evidence to incriminate Lady Dedlock. It also brings two other characters into the clutches of Tulkinghorn: Trooper George, as possessor of another document in Hawdon's handwriting, and the crossing sweeper Jo, an orphan befriended by Nemo. The pursuit of Jo as far as his deathbed, the reuniting of Trooper George with his mother, Mrs Rouncewell (Sir Leicester's housekeeper), and the eventual arrest of the true murderer of Tulkinghorn, constitute further subplots in this complex and mysterious novel. All these plots involve their various characters, and the reader, in a constant process of detection.

Detailed summaries

To economise on space the headline summaries for later parts of the novel treat complete instalments rather than chapters. Esther's chapters are denoted [E].

I (CHAPTERS 1–4)

CHAPTER 1 IN CHANCERY

In the heart of the London fog, the Lord Chancellor presides over a foggy court, which is diverted by a minor episode in the interminable suit of Jarndyce and Jarndyce

London. Implacable weather. Smoke. Accumulating mud. Dogs and horses and pedestrians indistinguishable in the mire. Cruelly penetrating fog. Gaslights. In the midst, the Lord High Chancellor presides over a foggy court, where lawyers, indistinguishable from each other, expound interminable briefs, floundering in the mud of an endless case, tripping each other up on slippery precedents, under a lantern with no light in it.

A little mad old woman awaits an incomprehensible judgement. A ruined suitor amuses the court by attempting to be heard. Mr Tangle makes a contribution to the matter of costs in the perennially hopeless case of Jarndyce and Jarndyce. The Lord Chancellor determines to settle the residence of two young orphans, the wards in Jarndyce. The court rises.

In this famous opening, the mud and mire of London **symbolise** the mud and mire of the law. The absence of finite verbs in the opening paragraphs suggests that action has no place in the Court of Chancery; the life of England is mortgaged to this place of despair. Words have taken the place of things; lawyers and court officials are described as (and might as well be) gowns, maces, bags and purses. The brief moment in which the Lord Chancellor attends to the fate of two anonymous young people, with a dead uncle, and a grandfather who has blown his brains out, startles with its sudden reality. As the following glossary shows, the imagery of the first few paragraphs establishes many of the novel's major themes.

Implacable ... weather what is 'implacable' cannot be placated; a major **theme** of the novel is the implacable pursuit of Lady Dedlock, or Trooper George

Megalosaurus a dinosaur; here, a **metaphor** equally applicable to Chancery, the Chancellor and 'Jarndyce and Jarndyce'

a general infection of ill-temper introducing the theme of disease

deposits ... of mud ... accumulating at compound interest the metaphor introduces the theme of money-lending, and, as most of the mud will be horse-shit, makes a Freudian association of money, dirt, verbiage and faeces

ancient Greenwich pensioners ... wrathful skipper ... 'prentice boy hints (only slightly misleading) as to the range of characters to come

Court of Chancery presided over by the Lord Chancellor, the Court of Chancery dealt principally in disputed wills and trusts, which lay beyond the competence of Common Law. Plaintiffs and defendants, whose disputes required the Chancellor to determine cases according to Equity, became victims of a protracted system whereby suitors could only be heard indirectly, that is via solicitors who would instruct barristers to present written evidence. Disputed property remained 'in Chancery' until judgement was delivered. Some especially infamous cases took decades to resolve

interminable brief a 'brief' can refer to a lawyer or to his written instructions, but here the **oxymoron** expresses the protracted futility of the law

the lantern with no light in it a round glazed window in the roof

the attendant wigs ... all stuck in a fog bank much of the energy of this chapter is purely linguistic, one word play leading to another; here a **metonymy** is stuck in a metaphor

silk gowns ... maces ... privy-purses parodying the law's own taste for metonymy (a silk is a barrister) these metonymies stand for dehumanised court functionaries

litter in a reticule ... paper matches it is implied that the litter in Miss Flite's handbag is as significant as the court's documents; her matches inaugurate the motif of combustion

This scarecrow of a suit a pun on legal suit and the threadbare dress of suitors

eighteen hammers in a piano-forte the barristers are indistinguishable components in a machine, a play on Thomas Carlyle's description of the period (in 'Signs of the Times', 1829) as 'the Mechanical Age'

Begludship compare Mr Tangle's strangulated language with the letter in Chapter 3

CHAPTER *2* IN FASHION

The world of fashion is not so different. Lady Dedlock, in her world, is quite as bored as the Lord Chancellor in his. Deadlock is common to both

My Lady Dedlock '(who is childless)' is bored to death. Looking out on the rain-sodden landscape of the family seat in Lincolnshire, she sees a child running out to welcome 'the shining figure of a wrapped up man' as he approaches the firelit windows of his cottage. My lady, the epitome of beauty and fashion, having been bored to death in the country, has now come to London, still bored, on her way to Paris where she will be quite as bored. Sir Leicester Dedlock, whose family is as old as the hills, is troubled by gout. A rusty old lawyer, Mr Tulkinghorn, as mute as the strong-boxes in his office, attends upon Sir Leicester and upon My Lady, who seems to have a remote interest (it is never explained) in Jarndyce and Jarndyce. Noticing the handwriting on a document in the case, her interest revives. 'Who copied that?' Too late, she screens her face from Mr Tulkinghorn's gaze. She faints.

> The **imagery** of mud and fog in Chapter 1 is echoed here, though in a muted style, in the rain and mist of Chesney Wold. Again as in Chapter 1, a sudden moment of human interest provides animation in the closing paragraphs. Who were the young people in Chapter 1? Why is My Lady's interest in this handwriting (though partly disguised by its acquired legal character) so great?

> As Mr Tulkinghorn reads, 'the heat is greater, my Lady screens her face' (p. 27). Two chapters have accustomed us to the vivid economy of this narrator's **metaphorical** style: clearly, it is not the heat of the fire that troubles My Lady. And why always 'My Lady'? Is the narrator both deferential and a little inclined to sneer?

Rip Van Winkles In Washington Irving's tale 'Rip Van Winkle' the hero slept through the American Revolution

The shot of a rifle the detail may be insignificant; but it echoes the shot which blew out Tom Jarndyce's brains (referred to twice in Chapter 1 and again in Chapter 3, and Chapter 8), and foreshadows another shot heard in Chapter 40, those fired in George's gallery, and the one that blows out Tulkinghorn's in Chapter 48

a baronet the lowest hereditary titled order, making its bearer very self-conscious about rank, as in Disraeli's novel *Sybil*

a Mercury the winged messenger of the gods; used throughout *Bleak House* to describe the servants of Sir Leicester in the Elysium of Chesney Wold

Wat Tyler leader of the Peasant's Revolt in 1381 at around the time the Court of Chancery was established. One of numerous revolutionary rumbles

CHAPTER 3 A PROGRESS [E]

Esther Summerson tells of her childhood, her schooldays, her mysterious benefactor, and how she became the companion of Ada Clare, one of Jarndyce's wards

In one chapter Esther takes us from her early childhood, with a severe godmother (Aunt Barbary) and an equally severe servant (Mrs Rachael), to her arrival in London. She is illegitimate, and is solemnly informed on her birthday that 'Your mother ... is your disgrace, and you were hers' (p. 30). After her aunt's death, Esther is placed at a school by a mysterious benefactor (Mr Jarndyce). From there, the same benefactor '*arrngd*' for her to be forwarded 'carriage free' to Kenge and Carboys and hence to the offices of the Lord Chancellor. There, screened from a raging fire, Esther begins her new life, as the companion of Ada Clare and her cousin Richard Carstone, the wards in Jarndyce. They run into a little mad old lady who mutters of the Day of Judgement.

The title 'A Progress' invites the question, progress of what? Hogarth's famous illustrated story, 'A Rake's Progress', or Bunyan's Christian allegory, *Pilgrim's Progress*, may be relevant. Also, whereas the **omniscient narrator** has taken two chapters to describe two brief moments in the deadlocked worlds of Chancery and aristocracy, Esther's narrative, despite its 'gush', does make progress: it sweeps in one chapter from infancy to employment.

The death of Esther's godmother (in reality her aunt) occurs while Esther is reading from the Bible the story of Christ intervening on behalf of the woman taken in adultery. Was Lady Dedlock an adulteress? The transition from Lady Dedlock's distress to Esther's (initially) anonymous narrative may suggest such connections. Several more transitions between these two narratives will link Esther to Lady Dedlock. What connection can there be?

One connection is in the **imagery**. Esther arrives in London in *fog*, meets immediately a young gentleman who has *inked* himself by accident (Guppy), meets Richard and Ada when *screened* from a raging Chancery *fire*, and seems remarkably in tune with the other narrator's sense of significant imagery, all these being key images on Chapters 1 and 2. Yet her approach to people is quite different. Even the Lord Chancellor seems affable in her presence, and is presumed to be human until proven otherwise.

the sins of others ... visited upon your head an allusion to Numbers 14:18, 'Visiting the sins of the fathers upon the children unto the third and fourth generations'. Jarndyce in Chapter 17 wonders whether the virtues of the mothers may not be visited likewise upon the children

St John ... 'Watch ye therefore!' Esther is reading the story of Christ intervening to prevent the stoning of a woman taken in adultery (John 8:1–11). Her aunt responds with an allusion to the second coming of Christ (Mark 13:35–7) and is probably thinking of the Last Judgment

'I expect a judgment. Shortly. On the Day of Judgment.' Miss Flite may be implying that Chancery decisions take an eternity, or that the end of the world is nigh

the sixth seal Miss Flite, the mad rhapsodist, associates the Great Seal of the Chancellor with the opening of the sixth seal in the Revelation of St John 6:12, portending calamities on earth

CHAPTER 4 TELESCOPIC PHILANTHROPY [E]

While Mrs Jellyby attends to Africa, her children perish. Esther rescues one and comforts the others

Mr Jarndyce has arranged for Esther, Ada and Richard to pass the night at Mrs Jellyby's, where Esther is astonished at the dirt and disorder to be seen everywhere in the household. One child has his head stuck in the railings, and is rescued by Esther; another falls down a flight of stairs; nothing works, Mr Jellyby is jellified, and the eldest daughter, Caddy, typifies the disorder. She is in 'a state of ink', with frayed slippers, and hardly an item of clothing 'in its proper condition or its right place'. Esther spends a sleepless night in which Caddy, asleep on her lap, merges sometimes with Ada, sometimes with the mad old woman. 'And I', says Esther, 'was no one' (p. 63).

Mrs Jellyby's showy philanthropy towards Africa contrasts with Mr Jarndyce's anonymous benevolence towards individuals in need (neither Ada nor Esther is conscious of ever having seen their benefactor). It also signals Dickens's (and Esther's) horror at mothers who mend the world while neglecting their children. But the severest criticism of the state of affairs is expressed by the neglected Caddy, whose childhood has been sacrificed to Borrioboola-Gha: 'I wish Africa was dead! ... I hate it ... It's a beast!' (p. 60). The **imagery**, from perishing stair-carpet to Caddy's frayed slippers, makes clear that London, Chancery, Chesney Wold and Mrs Jellyby belong to the same pattern of decay. Esther's sense of her own identity as 'no one' is one of innumerable but infinitesimal clues to her parentage.

Borrioboola-Gha modelled on a calamitous attempt to establish a philanthropic colony on the Niger in 1841

II (CHAPTERS 5–7)

CHAPTER 5 A MORNING ADVENTURE [E]

> **Esther's narrative leads to the rag-and-bone**
> **warehouse of the Lord Chancellor's parodic double,**
> **the eccentric 'Chancellor' Krook**

After washing Peepy and listening to an another explosion from the resentful Caddy, Esther finds herself again in Chancery, from which (Richard observes with unconscious **irony**) 'We are never to get out' (p. 66). Miss Flite, muttering of Revelations and the sixth seal, decoys them to her lodgings, a room in Krook's Rag and Bottle Warehouse. Esther describes Krook's collection of papers, torn-up gowns, empty ink bottles, bones, skins, and sacks of lady's hair; and, among all this, a notice – we may notice – in her father's hand. Krook has a liking for 'rust and must and cobwebs' as well as 'parchmentses' (p. 70). Uncannily, he forms on a slate the letters JARNDYCE, though unable to read or write, and names the suitors in the case. He has witnessed the suicide of Tom Jarndyce ('victim of rash action – brains' was Mr Tangle's account to M'lud in Chapter 1). Miss Flite's collection of songbirds is equally disturbing; the whole collection, imprisoned while Miss Flite awaits her judgment, 'has died over and over again' (p. 74). 'Ve-ry mortifying' is her chill comment.

The description of Krook's collection, and of Krook himself, seemingly 'on fire within', and boasting that 'all's fish that comes to my net' (p. 70), is Esther's first exercise in **symbolism**. Krook, coveting Ada's fine hair, and Miss Flite with her collection of caged birds, both symbolise the fate of all human victims of Chancery. Yet Miss Flite, too, is a tragic victim: 'I have felt the cold here. I have felt something sharper than cold' (p. 73). That is hardly surprising in a tenant of Mr Krook's macabre mausoleum (Esther feels that chill in Chapter 14).

The slow naming of Miss Flite introduces one of the book's repeated techniques. Many other characters (Jarndyce, Gridley, Jobling) appear once or twice before their identity is revealed. Naming has to do with the discovery of who one is (in Esther's case), and the uncloaking of characters and their secret purposes. Innocent of any such connection Esther passes by her father's door.

Lady Jane amiable, learned and clever (according to Dickens in *A Child's History*) the sixteen-year-old Lady Jane Grey was proclaimed Queen in 1553, resigned in favour of Queen Mary after twelve days, and was executed for treason by the same 'Bloody Mary'. So the cat's name *may* allude to perilous female empowerment. Or it *may* have the genital implication of 'John Thomas and Lady Jane'. Whatever her name signifies, however, the cat's powers of watching and rending signify the law

CHAPTER 6 QUITE AT HOME [E]

Esther and the two wards are welcomed at Bleak House by their eccentric benefactor, and exploited by his friend, the 'perfect child', Harold Skimpole

Approaching Bleak House by open carriage the young people are intercepted by a waggoner, with notes from Mr Jarndyce making it clear that any expression of gratitude will be unbearable to him. Esther realises from his voice that she has met him six years ago (when he threw a pie out of the window because she would not eat). His first response to their unease about Mrs Jellyby's neglect of her children is in the same phrase he used then: 'floored again'. His second is that 'the wind is blowing in the East'. Bleak House, with its brightness and warmth, its window seats and galleries, its irregular passageways and winding stairs is welcoming and comfortable.

They are introduced to Jarndyce's house guest, Harold Skimpole, as a perfect, undesigning child, a man of poetry and feeling, and quite indifferent to such sordid cares as money. Arrested for debt, within hours of their arrival, he allows Esther and Richard to rescue him with all Esther's savings and Richard's allowance. Mr Jarndyce feels the east wind again, until reminded by Esther that Harold is but a child. Jarndyce is so good a man, she reflects, that he is tortured by the thought of condemning, or mistrusting, anyone. Skimpole, on the other hand, mystifies her. How *could* he be so free from 'the duties and accountabilities of life'? Pondering these things, and her own origins, Esther goes to bed jingling her household keys.

> Esther's struggles to reconcile her own perceptions of Mrs Jellyby and Harold Skimpole with those of her guardian take many chapters to resolve. She is a minor, deeply indebted to Jarndyce, and with every reason to esteem him and look up to his judgement. Much of the power of Dickens's portrayal of Esther has to do with the difficulty she has, as a young dependent woman, and an illegitimate one at that, in learning to trust and express her own judgements. In this case, however, it goes deeper than that. Esther (jingling her keys) signifies responsibility and duty, and in Skimpole she has met her antithesis. A clear sign of Skimpole's monstrousness (there will be many more) is that he has the training of a medical man and puts it to no use.

Harold Skimpole Dickens based this character (rather unfairly) on the Romantic poet and journalist Leigh Hunt, the friend of Keats and Shelley. Hunt was certainly a sponger, and an aesthete, but also a man of principle and courage

CHAPTER 7 THE GHOST WALK

Mrs Rouncewell, housekeeper of Chesney Wold, shows Mr Guppy and his friend around the deserted house, and tells the story of the Ghost's Walk

What life and imagination there is in Chesney Wold (where it is still raining) belongs to the horses, dogs, rabbits and poultry, whose thoughts and memories the narrator probes. In the absence of the Dedlocks Mrs

Rouncewell presides, supreme in her world. She is troubled only by the memory of her long lost son, who 'went for a soldier'. Her other son, whose talents were of the steam-engine and hydraulic pump variety, went to 'the iron country farther north'.

Her grandson Watt (named after James Watt the industrial scientist) arrives; as does Mr Guppy with a friend. While Guppy and his friend inspect the house, under Mrs Rouncewell's guidance, Watt accompanies them to inspect the maid, Rosa, whose duty it is to explain the features of the house to the visitors. Mr Guppy thinks he recognises the portrait of Lady Dedlock, and becomes wholly absorbed in it.

As Guppy departs, Mrs Rouncewell tells the story of Sir Morbury Dedlock, a Royalist in the English Civil War, whose wife – childless and of a haughty temper – aided the Republicans. Lamed in the hip when attempting to lame Sir Morbury's horse, she slowly faded away, walking the terrace with her stick, and promising to haunt Chesney Wold 'until the pride of this house is humbled'. In time of sickness, or death (or disgrace, the impertinent grandson adds), the sound of the Ghost's walk is heard.

> Guppy's 'recognition' of Lady Dedlock is echoed by numerous characters, including Jo and trooper George, and we know already (from his appearance in her narrative) how attracted he was to Esther. His recognition parallels the way the narrative keeps passing from Esther to Lady Dedlock and back again. The chapter began 'while Esther sleeps': it ends 'So My Lady says'. Whose voice will open the next instalment?
>
> That the present Lady Dedlock, like her Civil war precursor, threatens to disgrace the ancient house, is signalled by the sound from the terrace now. The symbolism links sexual transgression with republican liberties (and as Dickens favoured republican liberties this has intriguing implications!).
>
> **Wat Tyler ... conspirators ... Watt** to Sir Leicester, industrial revolution and the peasant's revolt are equally unsettling. He associates factories with 'conspirators ... turning out by torchlight ... for unlawful purposes', a reference to the Chartist risings of 1842
>
> **the rebels who leagued ... excellent King** Mrs Rouncewell, a loyal retainer,

sees Charles I, executed in 1649, as 'that blessed martyr'. Dickens, in *A Child's History of England* says the people were martyred to his notions of divine right

III (CHAPTERS 8–10)

CHAPTER 8 COVERING A MULTITUDE OF SINS [E]

The sins covered in this chapter include Chancery and its blight on human lives, middle-class indulgence in fatuous causes, and Mrs Pardiggle's mode of 'rapacious benevolence'

Esther, now seeing herself as 'a methodical, old-maidish, sort of foolish little person' overawed by her responsibility for the tea-pot, visits the 'Growlery' where she first disgraces herself by kissing her benefactor's hand, and then learns what her role is to be. Jarndyce wants a trusted confidante, to 'sweep the cobwebs' out of their domestic sky. He unburdens his mind about the suit, and how after the suicide of Tom Jarndyce, he inherited the dilapidated Bleak House ('the brains seemed to me to have been blown out of the house too') and consults her about Richard's future.

A genuine philanthropist, Mr Jarndyce is plagued by innumerable false ones, among them Mrs Pardiggle. Scornful of Mrs Jellyby for excluding her family from 'the objects to which she is devoted', Mrs Pardiggle has conscripted her five disgruntled boys (and their pocket money) into her own charitable causes, teaching them 'charitable business in general'. Recruiting Esther and Ada she marches them off to visit a brickmaker's family, where, amid squalor, brutality and death, she erects an iron barrier between the visitors and the visited, taking 'the whole family into custody' like 'an inexorable moral Policeman' (p. 132).

Tactfully, Esther persuades Mrs Pardiggle to depart, so that she can offer some comfort. One battered wife, Jenny, is comforting another, whose child is dying. Esther responds powerfully to the sisterhood between two women, and 'what they could be to one another' in their shared trials. She covers the infant with an embroidered handkerchief, and returns later with 'some little comforts'.

CHAPTER 8 continued

Q. D. Leavis notes how the Chancery suit is treated as a **metaphor** for the human condition – in Jarndyce's words, we '*must* be parties to it whether we like it or not'. Jarndyce's character is much deepened in this chapter, and we see that his voice is capable of wrath as well as tenderness and affability. Describing the suit's London property as 'a perishing street of blind houses' and as bearing the impress of 'the Great Seal' he merges with the prophetic tones of the narrator and underwrites the seriousness of Miss Flite, another of the Great Seal's children.

This chapter establishes Esther as a brilliant observer in her own right, wonderfully responsive to Mrs Pardiggle's body language, and sensitive to each child's particular anguish. We can hardly suspect Esther of **irony**, but her basic principle of doing what kind services she can to those around her, and letting 'that circle of duty gradually and naturally expand itself' is Dickens's antidote to the brash, offensive, egotistical and rapacious 'benevolence' embodied in Mrs Pardiggle as an agent of middle-class virtue.

The battered wives, and their supportive sisterhood, reappear later in the novel. The association of drink and violence became a major feminist cause during this period, and is a frequent theme in Dickens. On the other hand, Mr Pardiggle is referred to only as 'O. A. Pardiggle, FRS … their father'. His scientific distinction as a Fellow of the Royal Society is subordinated entirely to his role as a minor contributor 'under my direction' to Mrs Pardiggle's causes.

Sisterhood of Mediaeval Marys a satirical reference to an Anglican Sisterhood founded in 1845 as part of the high church revival led by Pusey and his 'Oxford Movement'

the Females of America American women were in the vanguard of feminism

CHAPTER 9 SIGNS AND TOKENS [E]

Esther's main focus in this chapter is on Richard's financial recklessness, and his resentment at having to make his own way in the world, both signs of his likeness to, or infection by, Skimpole. A different kind of impetuousness is embodied in the character of Lawrence Boythorn, an implacable enemy of Sir Leicester Dedlock (over a trifling land dispute).

Boythorn's verbal explosions, however, are 'like blank cannons and hurt nothing' (p. 142), Esther says. She perceives his tenderness, as does his canary, and guesses that his hearty bachelor manner conceals a romantic spirit.

A scented Mr Guppy takes advantage of business with Mr Boythorn to speak to Esther, eyeing her in an unpleasantly 'scrutinising and curious way', and downing glasses of wine in rapid succession. He enumerates his advantages (salary, lodgings and a mother who 'has her failings ... but I never knew her do it in company' [p. 150]) before proposing marriage to Esther, whom he will love, honour and obey. Esther rejects his addresses with a haughty formality we have not suspected her to be capable of. When he leaves, she attends to matters of business for an hour, then laughs, then bursts into tears, feeling 'as if an old chord had been more coarsely touched than it ever had been since the days of the dear old doll, long buried in the garden'.

> Esther's determination not to write about herself, and the tendency of Jarndyce and Richard to regard her as a strangely sexless 'little old woman' are very prominent in this chapter. The same theme (of repression) is implied in Boythorn, whose sexual energies have been channelled into boisterousness. It recurs in Esther's response to the over-scented, wine-swilling, greasy Guppy and his grotesquely mismanaged proposal. We may be puzzled by Guppy's motives (does he love Esther, or does he bank on ferreting out her possible connection to Lady Dedlock?). More puzzling, perhaps, is her reaction. Her haughtiness is just like her mother's in later scenes involving Guppy. The reminder of the buried doll takes us back to what it **symbolised**. What did she really bury then? Hopes of being mothered? Of being loved? Of being a mother? Dickens wrote for family reading; his sexual implications are well concealed from the juvenile reader.

Boythorn the character of Jarndyce's oldest friend is based on Dickens's own friend the poet and essayist Walter Savage Landor

CHAPTER 10 THE LAW-WRITER

Tulkinghorn's pursuit of Lady Dedlock's secret leads him via the law stationer, Mr Snagsby, to the law writer, Nemo

Mr Snagsby's apprenticeship to Peffer led to a double partnership, one with Peffer, and one with his 'short, shrewd' and vinegary niece. One bone and one flesh, Mr and Mrs Snagsby are also one voice, mostly hers, especially when scolding the scullery maid Guster ('by some supposed to have been christened Augusta'). Mr Snagsby handles the professional side of the stationery business; Mrs Snagsby manages the money and Mr Snagsby. Not far from Mr Snagsby's shop are Lincoln's Inn Fields, where lawyers, including Mr Tulkinghorn, lie 'like maggots in nuts'. Mr Tulkinghorn, watched by a painting of 'Allegory, in Roman helmet' on his Neo-Classical ceiling, is contemplating a problem. Resolving it, he sets out 'as the crow came' to Snagsby's where he asks, very sharply, 'who copied this?' (c.f. Chapter 2, p. 26). While Snagsby accompanies Mr Tulkinghorn to Krook's, Mrs Snagsby does some sleuthing in the records. Mr Tulkinghorn eludes Mr Snagsby, and arrives in Nemo's room.

> The leisurely build up of the chapter seems designed to ensure that the instalment will end before we meet Nemo. A first slow movement is devoted to the Snagsbys (there is a moment of high comedy in the depiction of Mrs Snagsby, and especially her nose). A second, equally unhurried, movement is devoted to Tulkinghorn and his **allegorical** ceiling. In the third movement Mr Tulkinghorn's offhand conversation with Mr Snagsby disguises his steely purpose. Finally, a one-page description of Nemo's room tells us in nine or ten artful **metaphors**, recycling some of the novel's primary **images**, that the man Tulkinghorn thinks he has awakened is already dead. In plot terms, of course, this death is essential to sustaining the mystery: the death of Nemo frustrates Tulkinghorn just as the death of Krook in Chapter 32 frustrates Guppy. Otherwise the novel could end here.

> **Tooting** 150 children died in a cholera outbreak at a notorious orphanage in Tooting; Guster is, by implication, the damaged survivor of such a place
> **Banshee** supernatural being in folklore who warns of imminent death

IV (CHAPTERS 11–13)

CHAPTER 11 OUR DEAR BROTHER

Nemo's death leads to an inquest and a pauper's burial

Moments later (but a whole month later for the Victorian reader) a relighted candle confirms that Nemo's eyes are fixed in death. Tulkinghorn watches as the surgeon (Woodcourt) ascertains death, and Mr Snagsby (to avoid any suspicion falling on Tulkinghorn) is deputed to examine Nemo's belongings. Nemo has departed this life 'with no more track behind him, that any one can trace, than a deserted infant' (p. 173). Nor do we know if 'the now-extinguished fire within him ever burned for one woman who held him in her heart' (p. 179). An inquest gives opportunity for much comedy involving the neighbours Mrs Piper and Mrs Perkins, the local comic, Little Swills, and Mooney the Parish beadle (who, wishing to appear active and intelligent in the newspaper reports is reduced to anonymity as 'the active and intelligent' throughout the narrative). Mrs Piper and Jo the crossing-sweeper can tell the court nothing it wishes to know, but the latter attracts the immediate interest of Mr Tulkinghorn. Nemo receives a pauper's burial, in a beastly scrap of ground, 'pestiferous and obscene', where he is sown in corruption, 'to be raised in corruption', testimony to how 'civilisation and barbarism walked this boastful island together'. A belated mourner sweeps the step of the burial ground with his broom, and mutters his eulogy: 'he wos wery good to me, he wos!'

> Dickens lays on three virtuoso passages in this chapter. Mrs Piper's evidence '(chiefly in parenthesis and without punctuation)' displays the author's genius for mimicry through grammatical oddities and such word coinages as 'feariocious'. It must be read aloud. Jo's evidence, or rather the statement that determines the Coroner not to hear him, is based on the testimony of one George Ruby, reported in *Household Words* in 1850. The style, of compressed reportage of his answers to implied questions, is one Dickens used to equal effect in *A Tale of Two Cities*. The burial scene is heightened by the narrative voice engaging in sacrilegious **parody** of the prayer book, poetic prose suggestive of prophetic indignation,

and finally – in the paragraph of **anaphora** beginning 'Come night, come darkness' – echoes of Shakespearean soliloquy.

sow him in corruption, to be raised in corruption   negates the biblical 'sown in corruption to be raised incorruptible'
Come night, come darkness c.f. 'Come seeling night', *Macbeth* III.2.46

CHAPTER 12 ON THE WATCH

Mr Tulkinghorn watches Lady Dedlock's interest in Nemo while Hortense watches her interest in Rosa

Sir Leicester and Lady Dedlock (still bored) are expected home, where her portrait is touched by a 'bend sinister' of sunlight, which (signifying illegitimacy in heraldic designs) 'strikes down crookedly into the hearth and seems to rend it' (p. 182). Sir Leicester passes on from Mr Tulkinghorn a message to the effect that he has seen the law writer. The rooks engage in violent debate. Lady Dedlock is so interested in the nineteen-year-old Rosa that Mrs Rouncewell thinks it a pity she has no daughter. This interest arouses the wrath of My Lady's young maid, Hortense from Marseilles, with a watchful manner that is especially disturbing when she is anywhere near knives.

Chesney Wold is the haunt of what Dickens terms 'Dandyism' in religion and in politics, dangerously archaic yearnings, nostalgic for medieval retreat from the needs of the age. Mr Tulkinghorn, whose room allows him to stalk the leads about his turret, like a larger species of rook, arrives to discuss Mr Boythorn's disputes with Sir Leicester, and to scrutinise My Lady while reporting on the death of Nemo. Sir Leicester is disturbed, but only by the introduction of so low a topic as the death of a commoner in My Lady's hearing.

The long duel between Mr Tulkinghorn and Lady Dedlock, each reserved, and each suspicious, will occupy many chapters. Its conjunction with Lady Dedlock's interest in the nineteen-year-old Rosa reveals much of what remains unspoken.

Hortense is based on a Belgian murderess, lady's maid to the Duchess of Sutherland, who was hanged in 1849. She has been interpreted as the violent double of the frozen Lady Dedlock (Lady Dedlock sees Hortense's eyes when she looks into the glass) and of the repressed Esther (to whom Hortense offers herself in Chapter 23).

CHAPTER 13 ESTHER'S NARRATIVE [E]

Richard goes in for medicine, under the supervision of Mr Bayham Badger, and confesses his love for Ada

With the sceptical assent of Jarndyce, who is worried by Richard's procrastinating character, and the enthusiastic support of Boythorn, and the consent of the Lord Chancellor, Conversation Kenge arranges for Richard to 'go at' medicine, since he cannot settle on the army or the navy. His adviser, Mr Bayham Badger, shares his marital home with Mrs Badger and with portraits of her two former husbands Captain Swosser and Professor Dingo, their constant topic of conversation.

Meanwhile, Esther finds herself followed through her social life in London by a woebegone Guppy and finds his unwanted stalking deeply disturbing. Richard is pursuing Ada, who returns his love. He has to be cautioned by Jarndyce against entering an engagement to Ada until he is sure of constancy in love and in application to some means of supporting her. Esther's closing paragraph mentions that a young surgeon was present at the Badgers, and that she thought him very agreeable: 'At least, Ada asked me if I did not, and I said yes' (p. 214).

From the opening of this chapter the importance of Esther as Jarndyce's counsellor is stressed. 'We held many consultations' is her opening remark. She comments on the lamentable effects of Richard's classical education, and on the disturbing subjugation of Mr Badger to a woman of enormous vanity, much rouge and very few accomplishments. Her insight into the developing love between Richard and Ada makes it inevitable that Jarndyce, though much older, will appeal to her for advice and support in how he treats his two wards. That a young woman should be relied on in this manner is part of the gender dialectic of this novel. Yet Esther cannot admit to her own love interest as part of the story. Is the obsessive account of the tiresome Badgers there to disguise this unwillingness? The Badgers, Boythorn and Skimpole all become rather tedious. They would have been less tedious in serial form, but is it possible that Dickens *wants* the reader to tire of them?

V (CHAPTERS 14–16)

CHAPTER 14 DEPORTMENT [E]

Caddy Jellyby is to exchange her neglectful mother for an exploitative father-in-law

Richard depresses his friends by starting out on his new career in the wrong spirit – he is still looking to the suit to make him rich and save him the trouble of persisting in work. Caddy turns up with a still neglected Peepy, though she has done her best to make him presentable, and announces her engagement to 'Prince' Turveydrop, so christened by his father in honour of the Prince Regent. Mr Turveydrop senior is proprietor of a dance academy where he provides a model of deportment while his son does all the work. Esther is introduced to Prince who 'made this singular effect on me: that he was like his mother, and that his mother had not been much considered or well used'. This insight is confirmed by the mother of two pupils who informs Esther that Mr Turveydrop 'had worked her to death'. Esther herself is repelled by Mr Turveydrop's praise of herself and of Prince's 'sainted mother': ' "But Wooman, lovely Wooman", said Mr Turveydrop, with very disagreeable gallantry, "what a sex you are" ' (p. 229).

Caddy has been learning domestic management by helping Miss Flite, whose fortunes have been eased partly by a weekly allowance (anonymously given by Mr Jarndyce) and partly by the attentions of Mr Woodcourt, who has been her medical attendant since called to the deathbed of Esther's father. At Miss Flite's, where they meet up with Woodcourt and Mr Jarndyce, Krook recites the names of Miss Flite's birds. In his role as the Chancellor's double he watches Mr Jarndyce with the air of one who could divulge 'some secret subject', if he could make up his mind to do so. Esther reveals that Mr Woodcourt is the 'dark young surgeon' mentioned so coyly in Chapter 13.

> Mr Turveydrop, as Professor of Deportment, epitomises the **theme** of Dandyism, by which such characters as the aesthetic Skimpole and the aristocratic Sir Leicester are linked.

> Is it significant that Esther's distaste for Turveydrop's 'disagreeable gallantry' – especially combined with his exploitation of women –

occurs in a chapter when her awakening interest in Woodcourt is also prominent?

Krook may realise that his collection includes the document that will ultimately resolve the case of Jarndyce and Jarndyce, but only when 'my noble and learned brother' has extracted all value from it by due process of law. Krook, like Tulkinghorn, enjoys power; and like all the legal men, including Vholes and Guppy, he has a disturbing way of watching his prey, not unlike his cat's.

CHAPTER 15 BELL YARD [E]

The death of Coavinses, the bailiff, leaves three orphans, who are promptly visited by our friends

Esther offers a trenchant analysis of the suspect motives of organised benevolence, before passing to the mystery of Skimpole. She attributes her guardian's affection for him to his appearance of carelessness, contrasted with so much organised humbug, but she herself suspects him of politic calculation. Skimpole announces that 'Coavinses', the man who arraigned him for debt in Chapter 5 has 'been arrested by the Great Bailiff'. Discovering that the man was called Neckett, Jarndyce and Esther visit Mrs Blinder's house in Bell Yard where his orphaned children live. Tom and the baby Emma spend all day locked in a garret where, Tom says stoutly, it is sometimes 'almost quite bright', while Charley (aged thirteen) toils on their behalf.

A gruff fellow-lodger turns out to be Gridley, the Man from Shropshire (not heard of since Chapter 2). His irritation at visiting gentlefolk yields when Jarndyce (who never appears in court) reveals his name. Gridley utters a denunciation of Chancery as 'the System' (a *great* system, Conversation Kenge insists later) designed to suck away the livelihoods of the people. He vows to fight that system and unmask its individual agents until he dies. Skimpole discourses complacently on the poetry of life that makes people like himself the ultimate patron of Neckett's children, and enables Gridley, a man of natural combativeness, to exercise his combative energies.

Skimpole reveals a monstrous indifference to human suffering. One of Dickens's themes (borrowed from Coleridge) is that art may encourage false sentiment and real callousness, whereas the plight of these orphaned children brings out the genuine in the decent but very unpoetical Mrs Blinder, and the irascible Gridley.

Gridley may be seen as Jarndyce's double, as Krook is the Chancellor's. There is enough similarity between their passages of invective for us to see Gridley as an emanation of the Growlery – the dark side of Jarndyce. Jarndyce's whole life is a battle against being ruled by anger. But Gridley has brought Chancery down upon himself, by contesting a minor legacy to his brother, so his anger and pride ('I am not polite' is a constant boast) may contain much self-loathing.

CHAPTER 16 TOM-ALL-ALONE'S

What connection can there be between an ancient house and the whereabouts of Jo the crossing-sweeper?

While Sir Leicester is disabled by the family gout, My Lady is in London. In Tom-all-Alone's, where derelict houses can implode in a cloud of dust 'like the springing of a mine', bigger vagrants let space to lesser vagrants, all crawling like maggots in and out of gaps, bearing fever. Jo the crossing-sweeper, having breakfasted on the doorstep of the Society for the Propagation of the Gospel in Foreign Parts, wonders what the edifice signifies. Illiterate, ignorant alike of the meaning of shop signs and of the glories of the Constitution, he spends the day among the mud and wheels, to earn his nightly lodging in Tom-all-Alone's.

Mr Tulkinghorn, a greater maggot, sits in his chambers, wondering whether to arrest Gridley for menacing behaviour. A woman goes by. Why should he notice? 'There are women enough in the world … too many; they are at the bottom of all that goes wrong with it' (p. 259). Dressed as a servant but refined in manner the woman locates an astonished Jo, who shows her where Nemo died, where the Inkwhich was, and where he was 'berrid' in ground so shallow that they had to 'stamp on it to git it in'. Sir Leicester is restless. Mrs Rouncewell has never heard the step on the Ghost's Walk as distinctly as this night.

The connection between high and low, touched upon here, becomes an insistent **theme** in the novel. The revelation of Mr Tulkinghorn's true motivation, rank misogyny, is of at least equal interest. The problem for the reader is whether the novel confirms or contests that misogyny. Is Lady Dedlock sentenced to death for polluting a Norman house? Or is her rash action, in seeking the grave of her lover, in tune with the novel's desire that this **symbol** of patriarchy should fall?

VI   (CHAPTERS 17–19)

> **This instalment interweaves Esther's developing love interest, her confused 'recognition' of Lady Dedlock (she cannot admit to herself what her feelings mean), and Guppy's acquisition of two pieces of data – that 'a lady in a wale' has sought out the burial place of Nemo, and that Esther was left in Mrs Rachael's charge, before her arrival in London. As Esther stumbles toward recognising her parentage, Guppy stumbles toward acquainting Lady Dedlock with her living child**

CHAPTER 17 ESTHER'S NARRATIVE [E]

While Richard tires of medicine, Allan Woodcourt works long hours for little reward. Complaining that one day is too much like the next, Richard thinks of going in for law instead, to keep an eye on the case. Esther (whom Richard now nicknames Minerva, goddess of wisdom) advises him to be sure his mind is made up.

Jarndyce, hurt when Esther speaks of him as her father, tells Esther what he knows of her background. He dismisses illegitimacy as of no account, describing her aunt's decision to blot out all trace of her existence as the result of 'the distorted religion which clouded her mind'.

Allan Woodcourt takes his leave before setting out as ship's surgeon on a voyage to China. 'I believe – at least I know' and 'I think – I mean, he told us' is Esther's self-conscious way of registering this information. Mrs Woodcourt, his widowed mother assures Esther pointedly that no woman 'without birth' would be good enough for her son. Nevertheless,

Caddy presents Esther with a bouquet of flowers left at Miss Flite's, for Esther, by an admiring 'Somebody'.

> This chapter reminds one that this novel is largely 'about' the stigma of illicit love and illegitimacy, felt very deeply by illegitimates until well into the twentieth century. Does the strategy of having one narrative centred on 'fallen woman' and the other narrated by her child imply an attack on *both* stigmas?

CHAPTER 18 LADY DEDLOCK [E]

Months pass before Richard tries out Kenge and Carboy. His profligacy with money is contrasted to Skimpole's. Richard is all generosity and carelessness; Skimpole all calculation, only seeming careless. Visiting Chesney Wold, Esther is enchanted by what she sees as its serene repose. Boythorn's miraculous garden is described, prolific with apples, cherries, gooseberries, strawberries, peaches, marrows and cucumbers – all at once! In church, Esther is confused by Lady Dedlock's glance. She remembers standing tiptoe to look in her mirror as a child, and wonders why Lady Dedlock's face 'should be, in a confused way, like a broken glass to me'. The service comes to her in her godmother's voice, 'and *I* ... seemed to arise before my own eyes' (p. 292).

Skimpole and Boythorn pass the time in conversations on the edge of violent explosions, but the only acid response we hear is Esther's. When Skimpole speaks of slave plantations in the Southern States having a kind of poetry, Esther wonders in what light Mrs Skimpole and the children presented themselves to his mind (if he ever thought of them).

Near the keeper's lodge Lady Dedlock addresses Ada, and Ada replies 'O no, Esther dear'. We discover that Jarndyce was once a regular companion of Lady Dedlock and her sister, but not what this means. As Lady Dedlock returns home with Rosa, the displaced Hortense takes off her shoes and walks steadily through the wet grass as if, the keeper's wife suggests, she were walking through blood.

> Esther's response to Chesney Wold in the beautiful paragraph on p. 287 stresses its beauty, serenity and repose. Is this a naïve response compared to that of the **omniscient narrator** in Chapter 2? Or does her sense of its beauty expose the narrator's

view as jaundiced? Or is it that the two narratives, like Blake's *Songs of Innocence and of Experience*, express different states of the soul?

The emphasis on mirrors (here and elsewhere) appeals strongly to critics influenced by the psychological theories of Winnicott and Lacan. Briefly, we learn to see ourselves in the mother's face. Esther cannot claim her identity until she has a mother, having been cruelly denied any right to identity by her (wicked) godmother, a hopelessly inadequate substitute.

Slaves Dickens felt passionately about slavery; Esther feels similarly about domestic slavery; the equation is regularly made in the literature of women's emancipation

CHAPTER 19 MOVING ON

In London it is the hot summer vacation, and the lawyers are departed. Mrs Snagsby entertains Mr Chadband and his wife. Chadband, a preacher with a great capacity for turning comestibles into oil, breaks out into gusts of banal piety, 'piling verbose flights of stairs, one upon another'. A policeman consults Mr Snagsby about Jo, who refuses to 'move on' and who has about him two half crowns. Guppy is present by this time, and stays to cross-examine both Jo and Mrs Chadband. This produces the information that Mrs Chadband was formerly Mrs Rachael, servant to Aunt Barbary. Mr Chadband delivers an uplifting discourse on the unfortunate Jo – a suitable subject for improvement.

This chapter contains memorable examples of four of Dickens's most remarkable characterisations through speech: Chadband's banal oratory (vacuous and mellifluous), Mr Snagsby's helpless deference to his 'li-ttle woman', Guppy's virtuoso (and showy) cross-examination and Jo's poignant and perfectly honed illiteracy.

VII   (CHAPTERS 20–2)

How Guppy, though very small in the eyes of Kenge or Tulkinghorn, is a big fish in his own little pond, and employs Jobling as his eyes and ears; how the Smallweeds prey on the financially vulnerable, and thereby profit Mr Tulkinghorn; how Inspector

> **Bucket is retained for his own purposes by the same Mr Tulkinghorn. In short, how parasites shore up, and live upon, the underside of the great system**

CHAPTER *20* A NEW LODGER

Mr Guppy, smouldering at Richard's presence in the offices of Kenge and Carboy, takes a leisurely lunch with his admiring friends. The fossil imp Young Smallweed, fifteen years old and already an old limb of the law, wants to be a Guppy. Tony Jobling, whose hat and clothes have the appearance of a snail promenade, is out of work. Jobling tactlessly presses Guppy on his progress with Esther: 'there are chords in the human mind', retorts the pained Guppy. Lunch at Slap-Bangs is described in classic Dickensian style. Guppy, now familiar with Krook's through paying Miss Flite her allowance, and no doubt set on by whatever Jo was able to tell him about the law-writer in the previous chapter, installs Jobling at Krook's as his eyes and ears, under the alias of Weevle. He also stokes up Krook's inner fire with a bottle of prime gin. Jobling, who toured Chesney Wold with Guppy, and is an admirer of fashion, decorates Nemo's old room with copperplates from *The Divinities of Albion, or Galaxy Gallery of British Beauty* (among them, we find out later, Lady Dedlock).

> Little fish he may be, but Guppy's actions in this chapter are as purposeful as Tulkinghorn's in 'The Law-Writer', as the way he plays with his knife in the first paragraph suggests. The 'trusty Smallweed', despatched to see if Krook is at home, does not reveal that Krook is his uncle.

Divinities links up with the Mercuries, centaurs (coachmen) and other mythological hints
Albion an ancient name for England, used in William Blake's mythology

CHAPTER *21* THE SMALLWEED FAMILY

The Smallweed family is a little tribe of wizened monkeys with money on their minds. It is made up of the spindly Judy, sister to the elfin Smallweed, an infantine grandmother, perpetually falling asleep or into the fire, but waking up now and then to mutter of pounds and pence, and the irascible grandfather Smallweed. This patriarch is helpless in his lower limbs but savage in tongue and forever hurling cushions at Mrs Smallweed – 'you brimstone chatterer' – before collapsing like a broken puppet, until he is 'shaken up' and propped up again by Judy. They worship compound interest and are descended from a money-grubbing species of spider, whose business was trapping unwary flies. Their viciousness comes out in their exploitation and underfeeding of Charley (from Bell Yard) and their contrast with the healthy, soldierly figure of Mr George, a debtor, from whom Mr Smallweed extracts, every two months, a sum of money for his (imaginary) 'friend in the city'. Trooper George, it appears, might have done himself some good (in the money-grubbing sense) by helping Smallweed trace another debtor, Captain Hawdon. George makes his way home, jingling imaginary spurs, via the theatre. Home is George's Shooting Gallery, where the scorched and lop-sided Phil Squod, another orphan, keeps watch.

> The Smallweed domain is one of Dickens's most macabre comic creations, The heat from the fire ('you do well to get to used to one' says George), the constant references to brimstone (sulphur, the fuel of hell-fire) and the closing image of Mr and Mrs Smallweed as sentinels of 'the Black Serjeant' (death) all enforce the sense of this place as an entrance to hell.

> This chapter seeds later developments in Dickens. Dickens recycled the 'friend in the city' motif in *Our Mutual Friend*, and in *Hard Times* he developed the idea that vicious materialism results from strangling childhood imagination (no Smallweed has ever been young) as a major critique of Utilitarian philosophy.

> **'I'll lime you'** Smallweed's reference to liming (a way of trapping birds) emphasises George's free spirit, since birds **symbolise** imagination

CHAPTER 22 MR BUCKET

Allegory is cooling himself in the summer heat, the open windows fanning his rosy calves and peachy cheeks, while Mr Tulkinghorn releases from a bottle of fifty-year-old port the fragrance of southern grapes. With him is Snagsby, who has, as instructed, kept his visit from the watchful eyes of Mrs Snagsby. Mr Bucket (who was not there when Mr Snagsby entered and has not entered it since) materialises, and, as his name implies, dips down to the bottom of Mr Snagsby's startled mind. The object of this meeting is for Bucket to come up with information, via Snagsby, of the whereabouts of Jo, while impressing on Snagsby that discretion is imperative.

Together, taking a bull's-eye lantern from a constable, they enter hell, or rather a street of dark waters and fever houses, where people die 'like sheep with the rot'. Surrounded by a crowd 'like a dream of horrible faces' which fades away into the alleys emitting 'occasional cries and shrill whistles', the mysterious Bucket makes his way, constable by constable, to a lair in Tom-all-Alone's. They find two brickmakers in drunken sleep, and their wives. Liz, who comforted Jenny in Chapter 8, now has the bruises and the baby. Jo arrives, with medicine for Liz.

Leaving the fever houses, this 'concourse of imprisoned demons', Bucket leads Jo to Tulkinghorn who confronts him with the veiled figure of Hortense. This he identifies as 'the lady in the wale' until he sees her coarse hand and hears her coarse voice. Tulkinghorn promises to reward Hortense with a recommendation. Snagsby is amiably bound to silence by Bucket.

> This powerful chapter is built on several contrasts. Tulkinghorn's sensual relishing of expensive port, and the squalor of Tom-all-Alone's; Bucket's mysterious power and velvet persuasions, and the brickmaker's brutality; Snagsby's helpless sympathy and the sordid reality; power and powerlessness; manipulators and manipulated. The motifs of hell-fire and the **themes** of power and manipulation link all three chapters in this especially dark episode.

VIII   (CHAPTERS 23–5)

Hints of Hortense's capacity for violence, and an account of the death of the Man from Shropshire, share this instalment with Caddy declaring her engagement, more evidence of Richard's decline, and thematic comparisons of the egotism and self-absorption of Turveydrop, Mrs Jellyby and Chadband

CHAPTER 23 ESTHER'S NARRATIVE [E]

Before leaving Chesney Wold, Esther is astonished and rather frightened when Hortense offers herself as an unpaid domestic. Her intensity reminds Esther of 'some woman in the streets of Paris in the reign of terror'. Hortense explains that her barefoot walk in Chapter 18 was designed to remind herself of an oath (presumably, to have her revenge on Lady Dedlock).

Richard reminds Esther more and more of Miss Flite, and she finds him as little settled in the law as he was in medicine. Now he thinks of going into the army. Caddy and Prince kneel to Mr Turveydrop to announce their engagement, vowing to dedicate themselves to securing his little comforts. He promises grandly that in return for being kept, he will do 'all the rest'. Mrs Jellyby seems to have bankrupted the suicidal Mr Jellyby, who can make neither head nor tail of his affairs, but she is too busy to interest herself in her husband, let alone matters so insignificant as her daughter's engagement. Charley Neckett turns up as Esther's maid, 'a present' from Mr Jarndyce, who has also placed Tom at school and Emma with Mrs Blinder, delaying only to ensure that they could bear the separation.

> Those who see Mrs Jellyby as a malicious attack on feminism may like to note the direct comparison between herself and Turveydrop on pp. 380–1. Both parents are disappointed in their children. Prince, slaving for his father, is seen as merely useful but having none of his father's genuine deportment. Caddy, because she does not share her mother's absorption in Borrioboola-Gha, is of no account either. The engagement is between two victims of monstrous parental vanity. Is it appropriate to ask whether Jarndyce, benign and considerate in so many ways, also treats Charley as an object when he acquires her 'a present' for Esther?

CHAPTER 24 AN APPEAL CASE [E]

Now 'a vexatious and capricious infant' (p. 387) in the Lord Chancellor's eyes (and ours?), Richard becomes an ensign in the Horse Guards. He has exhausted his capital but still imagines he can rely on the suit for more. Jarndyce becomes estranged from Richard, having insisted that there be no engagement between him and Ada. Mr George, Richard's fencing tutor, thinks he recognises Esther. He reveals to Jarndyce that the customers at the shooting gallery have included Frenchwomen (Hortense?) and Gridley, who would come to the gallery and 'fire away until he was red hot'. Esther explains to George how they know Gridley. She visits Chancery, and reports on the case in progress – 'if I may use a phrase so ridiculous in such a connexion' (p. 397). Guppy introduces her to Mrs Chadband, who speaks 'with her old asperity'.

George arrives in search of Miss Flite to attend Gridley on his deathbed, now a shadow of himself. Bucket, having entered in the guise of a doctor in order to arrest Gridley for a breach of the peace, seems concerned for his old adversary and attempts to rouse him to some show of anger. Miss Flite's eerie scream marks the end of 'the only tie I ever had on earth that Chancery has not broken' (p. 406).

> Esther's maturity is seen in this chapter. She takes the initiative in conversations between Jarndyce and George; she sees Mrs Chadband for what she is; she scorns Chancery proceedings in her own right; she narrates a major death scene; and she perceives Richard's fate foreshadowed in the old woman and the dying Gridley.

CHAPTER 25 MRS SNAGSBY SEES IT ALL

Chadband takes Jo into moral custody yet again, discoursing upon 'the light of Terewth'. Mrs Snagsby's vinegary mind puts two and two together – her husband's secret disappearances, the mysterious lady and the ragged boy – and decides that 'Mr Snagsby is that boy's father'. Guster shares her supper with the ragged orphan. Mr Snagsby parts with a half-crown. Mrs Snagsby resolves to watch her husband henceforth, even more closely, in a grisly parody of the marriage service, 'bone of his bone, flesh of his flesh, shadow of his shadow'.

> As Turveydrop parallels Mrs Jellyby, Chadband is seen as a male Mrs Pardiggle, taking possession of Jo and labouring indefatigably but inappropriately for Jo's enlightenment. Meanwhile Mrs Snagsby joins the long list of characters engaged in detection.

IX (CHAPTERS 26–9)

Smallweed introduces George to Tulkinghorn and Guppy alerts Lady Dedlock to the identity of Esther

CHAPTER 26 SHARPSHOOTERS

While Leicester Square's socialites lie asleep, George and Phil Squod are up and about, Trooper George having a vigorous scrub in the icy water of the courtyard pump. They talk of Phil Squod's dreams of the country as a place of grass and swans 'a eating of it'; of George's being brought up a country boy; of Phil's running away from the parish with a tinker, and of his industrial scars, which include being scorched in a gas explosion. Grandfather Smallweed turns up, pleased with himself for turning Richard's debts to good account, and expecting more business in that quarter. As Tulkinghorn's agent, Smallweed asks George to provide a sample of Captain Hawdon's handwriting.

> The contrast between the wholesome Trooper and the avaricious Smallweed is further accentuated. Smallweed knows George is tutoring Richard, so he calculates that George will also incur more debts, relying on his new friends to bail him out. George's relationships are based on affection and loyalty; Smallweed's on turning people to account. The handwriting Smallweed wants will match the handwriting Lady Dedlock recognised in Chapter 2. As a further trace of interconnection, as yet barely visible, Richard is Sir Leicester's relation and George the son of his housekeeper.

CHAPTER 27 MORE OLD SOLDIERS THAN ONE

Waiting for Mr Tulkinghorn, George looks at the Chesney Wold boxes 'as if they were pictures'. Tulkinghorn offers to pay for a sight of any of the Captain's handwriting, to compare with Nemo's law-hand, and cautions George, who declines, to 'Take care you do no harm by this' (p. 436). George insists on consulting an old friend. Smallweed promises Tulkinghorn 'I'll twist him, sir. I'll screw him' (p. 437).

Outside a music shop George stops to contemplate its healthy, wholesome proprietor, Mrs Bagnet, who is washing greens. Mrs Bagnet not only washes the greens, and runs the shop, but is called on to deliver

CHAPTER 27 continued

Mr Bagnet's opinion on all matters, she being, decidedly, the mind of the partnership. The redoubtable Mrs Bagnet has made her way home to Europe, alone, with her grey cloak and umbrella, from another quarter of the globe; she has reared three barracks-born children, Quebec, Malta and Woolwich, and developed the family business from a total capital of sixpence.

When she delivers Mr Bagnet's opinion it is that George should never put his foot where he cannot see the ground; in short that he should have nothing to do with Mr Tulkinghorn's request. So George returns, and refuses. Mr Tulkinghorn, who knows that Gridley took refuge with George, calls Gridley as 'a threatening, murderous, dangerous fellow' (p. 445), which remark a passing clerk takes to be descriptive of George.

> Mrs Bagnet is one of the most formidable women in the book. Combining insight with decisive action she will rescue George from prison and reunite him with his mother. Dickens may approve of her only because (unlike Mrs Jellyby) she combines these qualities with dutiful washing of greens; but she is clearly Mr Bagnet's superior in such 'masculine' qualities as judgement, resourcefulness, decisiveness and commercial acumen.

CHAPTER 28 THE IRONMASTER

In Chesney Wold, Sir Leicester is enduring the visit of numerous dependent cousins who, being without state pensions or sinecures, live parasitically upon Sir Leicester. Among them, Volumnia Dedlock, a heavily rouged young damsel of sixty, and the Hon. Bob Stables, a crack shot. They discuss the shocking news that Mrs Rouncewell's son has been invited to stand for Parliament for the iron districts. Rouncewell is present, to speak to Sir Leicester and Lady Dedlock about Rosa, with whom his son Watt is in love. Mr Rouncewell wishes to remove Rosa, so that she can be further educated before marriage to his son, an idea profoundly offensive to Sir Leicester. The chapter ends with Lady Dedlock treating Rosa as a surrogate daughter.

> The dialogue between the Ironmaster, with 'his strong Saxon face' and Sir Leicester (consisting mostly of Sir Leicester looking magnificently indignant and Mr Rouncewell being dignified and sensible) dramatises the confrontation between the old aristocracy

of land and the new aristocracy of industry. The family fears that such obliteration of the social landmarks portends a general rising in the North of England. However ridiculous Sir Leicester's position, the narrator brings out his innate courtesy, and his sense of what he owes as host to his alarming guest.

CHAPTER 29 THE YOUNG MAN

In London, Sir Leicester is further discomposed by the announcement of 'a young man of the name of Guppy' claiming to have business with her Ladyship. Gallantly, he retires. Guppy, in a state of confusion to which his manners are not adequate, asks her lady point blank whether she noticed any family likeness in Esther. He tells her that Esther's aunt was Miss Barbary, and her real name Esther Hawdon, that a disguised lady went in search of Hawdon's grave, and that he can lay his hands on the boy who guided her. He has found out that Hawdon left a bundle of old letters, and claims that these will be in his possession 'tomorrow night'. He has ignored Lady Dedlock's stance of denial, confirmed in his suspicions by her pallor and by her reaction to the name of Hawdon. She tells him he may bring the letters if he wishes. Denying any pecuniary motive, he departs. Alone in her room Lady Dedlock – knowing now for the first time that her child lived ¬ gives way to wild sorrow.

> Reduced to confusion in the early part of his interview with Lady Dedlock, Guppy's motives remain ambiguous. Perhaps he merely intends to help Lady Dedlock. He is engaged in a race with Tulkinghorn, at some risk to himself. His gaucheness makes his manner half-threatening, and Lady Dedlock could be forgiven for taking him as a blackmailer, so it is much to her credit that her private reaction is grief rather than alarm: she cries 'O my child, my child' (p. 469), unlike a selfish person's 'What is to become of me!'

X   (CHAPTERS 30–32)

Mrs Woodcourt resumes her discouragement of Esther; Caddy's marriage takes place despite Mrs Jellyby's indifference; Jo arrives at Bleak House in a feverish state; Guppy fails to retrieve Lady Dedlock's love letters from Krook

CHAPTER 30 ESTHER'S NARRATIVE [E]

Mrs Woodcourt utters eulogies to Allan's lineage – which combines the blood of Morgan ap Kerrig with that of the Mac Coorts of Mac Coort – and prophesies that Esther will marry a much older man. All this seems contrived to discourage any romantic thoughts Esther may have regarding Allan. Arrangements are well advanced for stowing Caddy and Prince away cheaply above Mr Turveydrop's comfortable rooms, and for making Mrs Jellyby presentable at Caddy's wedding party. Mr Jellyby, after several attempts, makes his longest speech: 'Never have a Mission, my dear child' (p. 481). The wedding guests include the Pardiggles and Mr Quale, now the accepted suitor of Miss Wisk, who is a campaigner for woman's liberation from 'her Tyrant, Man'. All the guests talk uninterruptedly about their own missions, showing little interest in anyone else's. Mr Turveydrop promises never to leave his children.

> A wedding party is a somewhat **ironic** context for treating quite so many methods of bad parenting – Mrs Woodcourt, Mrs Jellyby, Mr Turveydrop, and Mrs Pardiggle.

CHAPTER 31 NURSE AND PATIENT [E]

Charley informs her mistress that Jenny and Liz, the brickmakers' wives, have returned, and that Liz has been seeking medicine for a poor boy. Jo has been so harried by 'Mrs Sangsby', that he has taken the 'Stolbuns Road', having heard of St Albans from Liz. Jo is terrified at the sight of Esther, whom he takes for Lady Dedlock, or Hortense. Liz has found no medical help for Jo, so Esther takes him home. When she consults Skimpole, as a medical man; he advises her to turn him out: 'The amiable face with which he said it, I think I shall never forget' (p. 495). A little later, when they have laid Jo in a loft room by the stable, Skimpole sings a touching ballad about a peasant boy, 'Bereft of his parents, bereft of a home'. Overnight, Jo disappears (why, we find out in Chapter 57). Charley catches the fever from Jo; and Esther, nursing her, contracts it in turn: 'I cannot see you, Charley; I am blind' (p. 504).

CHAPTER 32 THE APPOINTED TIME

In Lincoln's Inn, 'perplexed and troublous valley of the shadow of the law' (p. 504), there is 'a general tendency towards beer and supper'. Mr Snagsby, haunting the court outside Krook's, oppressed by the mystery he finds himself entangled in, discusses the heavy atmosphere with Mr Weevle, and finds it a little greasy. They attribute the smell and greasiness to chops at the Sol's Arms.

As Mr Snagsby departs, shadowed by Mrs Snagsby, Mr Guppy, who has been watching both, arrives. Admiring Lady Dedlock's portrait above the mantelpiece, Guppy and Jobling await the appointed hour at which Jobling is to receive the letters from Krook and pass them on to Guppy. Guppy tries to remove some soot from his sleeve but it smears. They debate what Krook may know about his accumulating documents. Guppy withdraws his hand in horror from the windowsill, covered in an offensive slime. In Krook's room nothing is found but oil, soot, a burning smell, and something else 'from which we [not *they*, but *we*] run away ... overturning one another into the street' (p. 519). Krook has died of Spontaneous Combustion, the death of all Lord Chancellors in all Courts, 'inborn, inbred, engendered in the corrupted humours of the vicious body itself' (p. 519).

> As an exercise in the slow accumulation of horror, this chapter should be sniffed, tasted and savoured many times. Its opening is analysed in Textual Analysis, Text 2.
>
> The dramatic style used for 'our' panicky exit, and the exaggeration and bombast about the deaths of all Lord Chancellors are instances of Dickens's unwillingness to be limited by the normal boundaries of fictional style.

The Appointed Time see Job 7:1

valley of the shadow of the law a play on 'Yea though I walk through the valley of the shadow of death' in Psalm 23

Spontaneous Combustion in the author's preface Dickens defends the scientific reality of such a mode of death, still debated from time to time

XI (CHAPTERS 33–5)

Smallweed takes possession of Krook's property, thus defeating Guppy; then, as Tulkinghorn's agent, he turns the screw on George by foreclosing on his debt. George has to hand over his piece of Hawdon's handwriting. Esther recovers, to find that a mysterious lady has visited St Alban's enquiring after her health

CHAPTER 33 INTERLOPERS

While Krook's death is investigated, Mr Snagsby, terrorised by a wifely eye, begins to think he may be guilty of 'spontaneously combusting' Mr Krook. As Guppy attempts to persuade Jobling to stay on the premises to discover its secrets, Grandfather Smallweed arrives to 'look after the property' and seal it up until Mr Tulkinghorn makes good the Smallweed claim. Men of science and the Coroner arrive to look at the scene of spontaneous combustion, and the defeated Guppy makes his way to Lady Dedlock to confess his failure. As Guppy leaves her Ladyship, Tulkinghorn arrives in time to perceive Lady Dedlock's embarrassment.

> Guppy's moment of triumph has been defeated not only by spontaneous combustion but by the hitherto concealed relationship between Smallweed and Krook. This has the potentially dangerous effect of advancing Tulkinghorn's interests, just as his observation of Guppy increases his suspicions.

CHAPTER 34 A TURN OF THE SCREW

Smallweed calls in Trooper George's debt, and thus exposes the Bagnets to ruin, because they have given security for his debts. Mrs Bagnet gives George a straight piece of Mr Bagnet's mind for involving them in such trouble. George and Matthew Bagnet fail utterly to soften Grandfather Smallweed, who refuses to renew their agreement, and smashes the clay pipe which George has smoked on each payment of interest. They proceed to Tulkinghorn's, where the lawyer is engaged with Mrs Rouncewell. As she leaves, Mrs Rouncewell notices the soldierly bearing of the two men, and speaks affectionately of her long lost son, while

George keeps his face to the wall. Tulkinghorn promises George that, in exchange for the sample of Captain Hawdon's writing, he will give a written undertaking that the Bagnets 'shall never be troubled in any way until you have been proceeded against to the utmost'. George cautions young Woolwich never to cause a sorrowful line in his mother's face.

> Two veritable children in this world of finance (as much 'babes in the wood' as are Richard and Ada in Chancery) the two old troopers are here established as touchstones of genuine innocence, by which the guile of someone such as Skimpole, as well as the malice and corruption of Smallweed and Tulkinghorn, can be measured.

CHAPTER 35 ESTHER'S NARRATIVE [E]

Esther's fever last many weeks. In her delirium she labours up colossal staircases, or seems to be one bead in a flaming necklace. As she recovers she finds that the mirror has been removed from her room, to protect her from the knowledge of her lost looks. Richard has broken off all contact, suspicious of Jarndyce as his enemy in the suit. Miss Flite, who has walked from London to St Albans in dancing shoes to see her, reveals that a mysterious lady with a veil has visited the brickmakers' cottage enquiring after Esther's health, and has taken away the handkerchief with which Esther covered the dead child.

Talking of her own affairs, Miss Flite agrees it that it would be much wiser not to expect her Judgment, or to attend court, but explains 'the cruel attraction of the place' and of the Mace and the Seal which 'draw people on', and draw the peace, and the sense and the good out of them. She tells how her father was drawn to bankruptcy and death, her brother to drunkenness, her sister to prostitution (it is implied), and herself into Chancery. She warns that Richard must be held back from destruction. Finally she reveals that heroism in a shipwreck has made Allan Woodcourt into a national hero. Esther is relieved that there was no understanding between herself and Allan, no relationship for her to break off, now she is disfigured.

> That Miss Flite is chosen as Esther's first visitor is partly a sign of Jarndyce's tact, in allowing her first social contact to be with

that 'poor afflicted creature', and partly a mark of how Miss Flite's significance is deepening, and partly a **symbolic** conjunction between two kinds of blightedness. Does Miss Flite's madness seems progressively less mad, her humanity more resilient, the more we know of the children of Chancery?

XII (CHAPTERS 36–8)

Esther's past and her new face are unveiled. She and Lady Dedlock meet as mother and daughter, for the first and last time. At ease with her new identity, Esther grasps that Richard's estrangement from Jarndyce is now total as he makes the suit the object of his life; she appraises Richard's predatory new lawyer, Vholes, approves Caddy's determination to progress from wife of a dancing-master to dancing mistress in her own right, and extracts from Guppy a promise to pursue her origins no further

CHAPTER 36 CHESNEY WOLD [E]

Convalescing at Boythorn's house, Esther gets used to her ravaged face, deciding to keep Allan's flowers only as a memento of 'what was irrevocably past and gone' (p. 573). She writes a letter for an old lady, and observes the tact with which a literate bride makes a mark in the register to avoid shaming her unlettered bridegroom.

As Esther enjoys the view of the Ghost's Walk, wondering about the ghost's figure, Lady Dedlock materialises. Esther's reaction to Lady Dedlock's motherly tenderness is a burst of gratitude that there is no longer 'any trace of likeness' (p. 579) and she accepts her mother's decree that if she is not to disgrace her husband they can never associate in this life. Lady Dedlock reveals her dread of Tulkinghorn, whose calling is 'the acquisition of secrets, and the holding possession of such power as they give him' (p. 581). She describes her belief that her child had never breathed (is this quite consistent with the earlier account?). Esther, crying to find herself a burden to the world, finds herself on the Ghost's Walk, and 'Seized with an augmented terror of myself' (p. 586) retraces her steps. She knows that she was 'as innocent of my birth, as a queen of hers'

(p. 587) and the shadow of her godmother's words has passed. Yet she awaits Ada's arrival in real terror that her darling's expression will betray something other than fondness and affection.

> The psychology of this chapter is fascinating. The parallel between Esther's relief that she had no relationship with Allan to break off, and her relief that nobody now will notice her likeness to her mother, suggests a deep and calm disinterestedness. This sense of empowerment coexists, however, with an identity so fragile that it might be shattered by any change in Ada's feelings towards her.

> There is a surcharge of melodrama in the treatment of Lady Dedlock's belief that she must pursue a 'dark road' through a 'desert', alone and 'conscience stricken', towards her 'doom': are we meant to ask why? Should we question her belief that Heaven can never forgive her? If Sir Leicester can (as he will, in Chapter 58) why not Heaven? If the novel *does* condemn her, is it as a fallen woman, or for making this scene the only 'natural moments of her life'?

CHAPTER 37 JARNDYCE AND JARNDYCE [E]

Richard visits Chesney Wold, incognito. His decency comes out in his unchanged warmth to Esther, when she puts up her veil. That she has developed comes out in her straightness with him over his new enmity toward Jarndyce. She cannot see any proof of unworldliness in Skimpole's sponging on Richard, and she insists to Skimpole that he, like everyone else, is obliged to be responsible. Richard, who suspects Jarndyce of discouraging him for selfish reasons, has now determined to make the suit the object of his life. Ada (who is still a ward, whereas Richard is of age) begs him in a letter to turn his back 'upon the shadow in which we both were born' (p. 602).

Richard's new lawyer, Vholes, to whom Skimpole has introduced Richard in return for commission, is described by Esther in chilling terms. He has cold lips, but red eruptions on his face, is black gloved, with an impaired digestion, and has 'a slow fixed way' of looking at Richard. He drives Richard 'away at speed to Jarndyce and Jarndyce' behind a pale horse. Ada, the prospective angel in the house, vows never to think of herself if she could devote herself to Richard, or think of her own delights if she could minister to his.

Chapter by chapter Esther, though still vulnerable, is gathering forcefulness. It comes out not only in her handling of Richard and Skimpole (who now recognises her as 'the very touchstone of responsibility' [p. 603]), but in her masterful portrayal of Vholes. In Chapter 5 she stumbles on Krook's characteristics, but in this chapter she depicts Vholes's predatory qualities with great deliberation.

CHAPTER 38 A STRUGGLE [E]

Esther visits Caddy Jellyby in her new life, and remarks that she always called Caddy by her maiden name. Caddy has formed the significant ambition to progress from dancing-master's wife to dancing mistress. Mr Turveydrop has accepted both Mr Jellyby and Peepy. To one he discourses upon the Prince Regent; the other he sends on errands, rewarding him with the occasional crust.

Esther visits Mr Guppy and his mother (whose comical behaviour, Guppy says, 'though highly exasperating to the feelings, is actuated by maternal dictates' [p. 615]). Esther, putting up her veil, is demoted instantly from the 'image imprinted on my heart' to 'a shattered idol' from whom he is estranged 'by circumstances over which I have no control' (p. 616). Esther extracts from him a promise (honourably given) that he will pursue her past no longer. Guppy, in a scene of high comedy, insists on Caddy witnessing, with full pomp and legality, Esher's full admission that there never was any engagement between them, and that circumstances rule out any recurrence of 'the tender passion'.

Esther, having tested the quality of love she enjoys from her mother, Jarndyce, Miss Flite, Charley, Caddy, Ada and Richard, and found them proof against any change of affections, seems able to enjoy the shallow Guppy's utter confusion. The next test, in Chapter 45 will be more difficult. Arguably, of course, the fact that she makes people's reactions to her new face the centre of so many chapters is a sign of egotism – readers often blame her (rather inconsistently) both for her early reticence and for her later self-absorption.

XIII   (CHAPTERS 39–42)

> As Vholes and Skimpole eat into his substance,
> Richard is persuaded that Jarndyce is his adversary;
> smouldering combustion takes hold. In the gloom of
> Krook's shop Mr Tulkinghorn watches as Guppy
> tries to discover whether any papers remain. In a
> general election Mr Rouncewell's candidate beats Sir
> Leicester's. Tulkinghorn demands that Lady
> Dedlock, whose secret he now knows, continue to
> play her part until he decides what to do with her. He
> threatens Hortense with the treadmill

CHAPTER 39 ATTORNEY AND CLIENT

In his burrow-like offices, the respectable Vholes goes about his cannibalistic practice of 'making hay of the grass which is flesh' (p. 621). As Skimpole watches, Vholes quietly fans Richard's smouldering resentment of Jarndyce, for wishing to strangle the suit, and extracts from him a further instalment of costs. We have our shoulder to the wheel, Vholes assures him, and the wheel is going round. As Vholes raps his desk, which sounds as hollow as a coffin, he assures Richard that it is his rock. As the client writes a draft for twenty pounds, Vholes watches him and the 'official cat watches the mouse's hole' (p. 629). Leaving Vholes's chambers, Richard is observed by Guppy and Jobling. The latter sees in him a clear case of 'smouldering consumption'.

Guppy and Jobling make their way to Krook's, where the Smallweed family sift through the graveyard of papers. Guppy, faithful to his promise to 'the shattered image', hopes to catch a sight of Lady Dedlock's letters so that he may burn them. But the watchful Tulkinghorn emerges from shadows. He congratulates Guppy on his access to elegant ladies, and comments that Jobling's picture of Lady Dedlock is 'A very good likeness in its way, but it wants force of character' (p. 637).

Vholes's cat seems an appropriate **symbol** for a chapter in which Vholes and Skimpole, Guppy and Jobling are all watching Richard, while Tulkinghorn watches Guppy watching the Smallweeds, who are scrutinising Krook's 'remains'.

CHAPTER 39 continued

> **the grass which is flesh** c.f. 'all flesh is as grass', I Peter 1:24. Christ called
> on Peter the fisherman to be 'a fisher of men', so this reference to Vholes
> as a harvester of flesh, links back to Krook's 'all's fish that comes to my
> net' (Chapter 5)
> **the wheel ... Ixion** Ixion in Greek mythology was bound to a wheel of fire

CHAPTER 40 NATIONAL AND DOMESTIC

The ship of state has been unpiloted for some weeks because Lord
Coodle 'would go out' and Sir Thomas Doodle would not, at first, 'come
in'. Seeking a majority, Doodle throws himself on the country 'chiefly in
the form of sovereigns and beer'. Sir Leicester's party, despite its control
of numerous rotten boroughs, has spent hundreds of thousands of pounds
on 'necessary expenses' (not to say bribery) to ensure the continuance of
Doodleism. Worse, Mr Tulkinghorn reports that, in a contested seat, Mr
Rouncewell's candidate has triumphed over Sir Leicester's. The
debilitated (i.e. sloshed?) cousin thinks this is the sort of thing 'that's sure
tapn slongs votes – giv'n – Mob' (p. 647) (i.e. in a democracy). Sir
Leicester thinks 'the floodgates of society are burst open' (p. 648), and
moreover, that Rosa should be kept from the influence of such people.
Such people, Mr Tulkinghorn observes 'are, in their way, very proud'
(p. 649), at which Sir Leicester 'doubts his hearing'. Mr Tulkinghorn tells
the gathering a cautionary story of how a townsman of Mr Rouncewell
removed his daughter from the employment of a great lady once it
became known that the lady had, in her youth, given birth to the
illegitimate daughter of an army captain.

> **an auriferous and malty shower** an elegant **periphrasis** on 'sovereigns and
> beer', with the additional piquancy of a classical allusion (Jove visited
> Danae in the form of a shower of stars)

CHAPTER 41 IN MR TULKINGHORN'S ROOM

In his room Mr Tulkinghorn savours his recent display of power. Lady
Dedlock enters to ask whether she can save Rosa before her guilty secret
is revealed. He is noncommittal. She speaks of leaving that night. He
insists that she stay, and continue exactly as usual, until he has decided
what to do and how to prepare Sir Leicester for the blow. Sir Leicester,
'the family credit', the baronetcy, and 'his patrimony' are Tulkinghorn's

sole concern. Flight, with the effect on Sir Leicester and the scandal it would cause, 'is not to be thought of'. When he decides to expose her, she will receive due warning.

CHAPTER 42 IN MR TULKINGHORN'S CHAMBER

Snagsby visits Tulkinghorn in a state of anxiety about the fact that Hortense has been haunting Cook's Court, and provoking speculation among the neighbours as well as Mrs Snagsby. Hortense arrives in Tulkinghorn's office and accuses him of shabby behaviour. She has been paid, he insists. She produces the two sovereigns and flings them away: 'I ref-use them, I des-pise them'. She demands that he help her to find a position, or employ her to disgrace and dishonour Lady Dedlock. Tulkinghorn reminds her that 'In this city, there are houses of correction (where the treadmills are, for women)' (p. 667) and promises 'what I threaten, I will do' (p. 668).

> The term 'patriarchy' was not used in its modern feminist sense (implying male oppression of women, as opposed to a system of government by tribal patriarchs) until very recently, and is not used in this novel. But Tulkinghorn's defence of 'patrimony' (property inherited from one's ancestors), associated with his view that marriage is the cause of three-fourths of the world's troubles, may imply a fierce commitment to male dominance. Here he seems to relish torturing, controlling and threatening two women in three successive chapters – quite as much as he relishes his port. Could Dickens be **symbolising** 'patriarchy' in an extreme form?

XIV   (CHAPTERS 43–6)

Esther perceives that Skimpole exploits his own family as much as he exploits Richard. She accepts a proposal of marriage. Allan Woodcourt returns and takes first Richard, then Jo, under his wing

CHAPTER 43 ESTHER'S NARRATIVE [E]

Ada and Esther ask Jarndyce to stop Skimpole 'advising' Richard, Esther pointing out that he introduced Richard to Vholes for five pounds. They visit Skimpole's dilapidated house, and warn him that Richard is not rich.

Jarndyce still thinks Skimpole is an artless child, and even Esther is half persuaded in his company, yet she hates to think 'of his having anything to do with anyone for whom I cared'. They meet his Beauty daughter, his Sentiment daughter, and his Comedy daughter. Like Caddy, the Beauty daughter, her husband and their fledglings 'have their nest up-stairs'. The three daughters have 'grown up as they could', with 'as little hap-hazard instruction as qualified them to be their father's playthings in his idlest hours' (p. 677). Jarndyce gives the invalid Mrs Skimpole a little money. As they leave, Esther observes that Skimpole's own apartment 'was a palace to the rest of the house'.

Sir Leicester calls, to regret that, because of Boythorn's enmity, Mr Skimpole, a gentleman of cultivated taste, did not have the pleasure of calling at Chesney Wold. Jarndyce and Esther exchange confidences: that her aunt was Lady Dedlock's sister, and that the same sister was the woman Mr Boythorn was to have married. Esther's burden of guilt is increased, but Jarndyce assures her of her innocence. She wonders how she can ever show him how 'I blessed and honoured him' (p. 686).

CHAPTER 44 THE LETTER AND THE ANSWER

Jarndyce asks Esther to consider whether she is assured that nothing can change his conduct towards her, then asks her to send Charley to him after a week, for a letter. The letter asks her to become 'the mistress of Bleak House'. It says (she feels) all that it should say, without hinting at either her birth or her disfigurement. Esther is grateful, yet experiences a sense of loss. She burns Allan's flowers, and waits for two weeks, during which time Jarndyce never mentions 'the letter'. Finally she approaches him and says yes. But 'it made no difference presently ... and I said nothing to my precious pet about it' (p. 694).

> For the modern reader this is one of the oddest chapters in the novel. It may help to remember: (1) that Jarndyce is conscious of the time when Ada will leave and it will no longer be possible for Esther to remain with him on other than married terms (though as it turns out, she does); (2) that to apply any emotional pressure to her would be a violation, because he has been her guardian, and has nowhere else to go; and (3) that, in the social conditions of a Victorian household, he has no other way of giving her time and

space to reflect. At the same time, her low-key response suggests that she accepts out of a sense of gratitude and obligation. Does her failure to tell Ada signify that she is deeply unsure, and perhaps ashamed?

CHAPTER 45 IN TRUST

Mr Vholes arrives at Bleak House to tell Jarndyce that Richard is in financial difficulties, and may be about to leave the army. Esther travels to Deal, overnight, with a letter from Ada, offering Richard her inheritance. Richard's response is that the offer probably comes with Jarndyce's connivance, as a means of buying him off. He is weary of the army, and unwilling to leave the 'case' in Vholes's hands. Among the passengers disembarking from a large Indiaman, Esther recognises Allan Woodcourt. She retreats to her hotel, where she hears him arrive, and sends a card telling him of her presence. Allan seems distressed for her, and he accepts from Esther, as 'a trust', the task of being a friend to Richard, who is proposing to lodge with Vholes.

> Esther's actions in this chapter – making her own decision to travel to Deal, with only Charley as a companion, contacting Allan, putting up her veil – are all indicators of gathering self-confidence, though she is wrong in her reading of Allan.

CHAPTER 46 STOP HIM!

Tom-all-Alone's continues to propagate infection and contagion, which can reach out to the choicest stream of Norman blood, working its retribution on even the highest of the high. Allan Woodcourt tends a bruised woman (Jenny). Leaving her he notices an emaciated boy, who seems familiar (Allan remembers Jo from the Inquest on Nemo). A moment later, the boy is running away from the woman. Allan stops him, and Jenny identifies Jo, whom she has not seen since he carried the fever to St Albans, and to Esther. Allan fights against a sudden revulsion. Jo explains that he was taken away from Bleak House by Bucket (whom he is frightened to name) who put him in a 'horspittle' and told him to make sure he never came within forty miles of London. Allan leads him out of Tom-all-Alone's to find him a refuge.

The opening reference to interconnectedness is continued in the chance encounter between Allan, Jenny (who will later change places with Lady Dedlock) and Jo, who carried infection to Esther. Mr Bucket, Jo's pursuer, will eventually pursue Lady Dedlock, and he is acting directly or indirectly for Sir Leicester in both cases. Allan's concern, of course, is the antithesis of society's neglect.

XV   (CHAPTERS 47–9)

Jo dies at the shooting gallery, tended by Allan Woodcourt and Phil Squod. Lady Dedlock sends Rosa away, incurring the wrath of Tulkinghorn. Tulkinghorn is murdered. At Mrs Bagnet's birthday party, the amiable Bucket becomes so fond of Trooper George that he takes him into custody

CHAPTER 47 JO'S WILL

Jo draws his breath 'as heavy as a cart' (p. 720). Knowing that finding an official refuge for him will be very hard, Allan gives him a little breakfast, and leads him gently to Miss Flite, who decides that 'General' George will help. George offers to take Jo in, and Phil Squod, found in a gutter himself, takes charge of getting him a bath and some clothes. The Trooper identifies Tulkinghorn's as the office to which Jo was taken at the beginning of his ordeal, and describes the lawyer as 'a slow-torturing kind of man' (p. 727), whom he would happily ride down in a field of combat. Jarndyce warns Allan that Jo's presence must be kept secret. Jo refers so often to Mr Snagsby that Allan sets off in search of him. Snagsby, though much alarmed to find himself once more caught up in mystery, visits the gallery and lays out innumerable half crowns while Jo asks him to write out 'very large' how sorry he was to have harmed Esther. With Jarndyce in attendance, Jo's cart reaches the end of its road, as Allan leads him through the Lord's prayer.

> Some nineteenth-century readers thought the death of Jo one of the high points in English literature. Modern readers find it sentimental in the extreme, but the sentiment has a purpose. Throughout this scene Dickens indicts his society for the lack of any welfare system for home-grown destitutes such as Jo, the

irrelevance and self-regard of Chadband and other merchants of religion, and the failure of her Majesty, and of 'Right Reverends and Wrong Reverends of every order' to deal with the plight of those are not only suffering in their midst but 'dying thus around us, every day'. There is, as Graham Storey has noted, a delicate allusion to *Othello* in the reference to Phil Squod laying aside his hammer so as not to disturb Jo: 'When the little hammer is next used, there will be a speck of rust upon it'.

CHAPTER 48 CLOSING IN

Mr Rouncewell calls at the house in London, where Sir Leicester receives that 'ferruginous person' with unaltered graciousness. Lady Dedlock (after a touching scene with Rosa) informs the iron gentleman that she wishes him to take Rosa away. Mr Tulkinghorn, who has witnessed this scene, is furious that Lady Dedlock should break their agreement by acting (as he sees it) in this untoward way. He informs her that she will receive no further notice of her doom. As Mr Tulkinghorn arrives home, Lady Dedlock slips out of the house. In Lincoln's Inn Fields a shot is heard. In the morning, Allegory points down at a bottle of wine, a glass and a stain upon the floor, where Mr Tulkinghorn lay all night, face down and shot through the heart.

> The murder is set up so as to ensure that the reader's suspicion is likeliest to fall upon either Lady Dedlock or Trooper George, as those with the clearest motive and most pronounced detestation of the lawyer.

CHAPTER 49 DUTIFUL FRIENDSHIP

It is the old girl's birthday, and Mrs Bagnet spends it in her customary anxiety as Mr Bagnet acquires the toughest specimen of poultry imaginable, and superintends its roasting. George, still distressed at the death of Jo, arrives for his evening smoke and drink. The recent death recalls Gridley to mind, and the 'flinty old rascal' (Tulkinghorn) who had to do with both. Bucket calls, and talks of his desire to find a second-hand cello, compliments the children and the parents, admires the backyard (and the fact that there is no way out), appreciates Woolwich playing the fife. He is generally the life and soul of the party. He cements a friendship with the entire family, and then, as soon as they are alone, arrests George for the murder of Tulkinghorn.

> Bucket seems to enjoy the wholesome company, and to have a real regard for domesticity. At Gridley's deathbed he also seemed genuinely concerned, as he did for Jenny and Liz in Tom-all-Alone's. Yet Bucket is a deeply ambiguous character. It is hard to feel confident that George will survive this arrest. Does Bucket serve decency and justice, or authority and power?

XVI   (CHAPTERS 50–3)

> **Esther sets aside her feelings for Allan Woodcourt.
> Ada acts upon hers for Richard. George stolidly
> awaits his fate in prison, obstinately refusing legal
> help. Bucket completes his case against the murderer
> of Tulkinghorn**

CHAPTER 50 ESTHER'S NARRATIVE [E]

Caddy falls ill. She has a small and listless baby, called Esther, whose dark veins seem like marks of Caddy's inky past. It is Ada's twenty-first birthday, and Woodcourt is expected to dinner. As Ada knows of Esther's feelings for Woodcourt, Esther feels she must tell Ada that she has agreed to become the mistress of Bleak House. Visiting Caddy, Esther notes again the contempt of Mrs Jellyby for her daughter's and Esther's 'limited sphere of action' (p. 772) and Mr Turveydrop's parallel condescension to his family as their benefactor. Mr Jellyby and the thoughtful baby seem to understand each other. Woodcourt's attendance on Caddy revives her. Esther absents herself when he is expected, pleased (she says) to think that he pities her, rather than loves her. Mr Jarndyce suspects that Woodcourt will emigrate, having experienced some unspoken disappointment in the old world. Esther, still troubled by a sense that something is reserved between herself and Ada, notices that she sleeps with her hand hidden under the pillow.

> This quiet chapter is very subtle in its handling of Esther's state of mind. She speaks of her confession to Ada as 'casting this last idle

reservation away' (p. 771), and of having hardly realised that it was a reservation, and wonders whether Ada is 'a little grieved – for me' (p. 775). At the close of the chapter she accuses herself of egotism in assuming that the shadow between herself and Ada has to do with her own secret engagement to Jarndyce, and that 'it only rested with me to put my dear girl right' (p. 778).

CHAPTER 51 ENLIGHTENED [E]

A few weeks earlier, Allan had visited Vholes, seeking Richard's address, while Vholes dropped several clear hints that Richard's friends may need to contribute to his costs. Richard claims that his life has 'an object now – or it has me' (p. 781). To his credit, he contrasts Allan's ability to put his hand 'upon the plough, and never turn' (p. 781) with his own vacillations. Ada leads Esther directly to Richard's lodgings, while dissembling any knowledge of that address. Esther observes the forced quality of Richard's belief in Vholes's assurances of progress. Ada admits she is 'not going home again' (p. 789) and that they have been secretly married for two months. Esther returns home, desolated. Jarndyce, who has just returned from Jo's deathbed, intuits immediately that Ada has married. He is still 'fatherly' and Esther fears that she has not been all that she meant to be, 'since the letter and the answer'.

> The continuing sense of reserve in Esther's commitment to her engagement, and her unease about the relationship being unchanged by 'the letter', is a major theme of this chapter. A more striking one is Ada's disobedience. In marrying without her guardian's permission, and while still under age, the apparently meek and submissive Ada has defied Jarndyce's authority as legal guardian and as a man. Yet neither Jarndyce nor Esther makes anything of it. More surprising, perhaps, in a novel much concerned with gender stereotypes, is that Jarndyce's 'intuition' tells him immediately what Esther's had not. What else has his intuition told him?

CHAPTER 52 OBSTINACY [E]

Woodcourt brings news of George's arrest and explains how appearances are against the Trooper, but Jarndyce asserts his belief in the innocence of this open-hearted gentle giant. They visit his prison cell and Jarndyce is astonished to find that George speaks of his plight with complete indifference and refuses the aid of a lawyer. He refuses any defence but his innocence. Knowing that truth is not enough, Jarndyce is appalled. George mentions that on the night of the murder he saw a shape like Esther's, in a loose mantle with a deep fringe, go past him at Tulkinghorn's. Outside, having signified that she wants a conference, Mrs Bagnet recalls how, after a visit to Tulkinghorn, George had spoken tenderly of motherhood. There and then, to everyone's amazement, she pins up her skirts and strides away to Lincolnshire, to fetch George's mother.

> A sentence you might like to think about is this: ' "Now, I tell you, miss," said Mrs Bagnet; "and when I say miss, I mean all!" ' (p. 801). In nineteenth-century discourse the male subsumes humanity, and women are 'relative creatures'. In Mrs Bagnet's world, men are 'relative creatures'. 'Miss' includes not only Mr Bagnet, who is always subsumed under Mrs Bagnet, but also Mr Woodcourt and Mr Jarndyce.

CHAPTER 53 THE TRACK

Mr Bucket's forefinger is very busy, as Mr Tulkinghorn's funeral is attended by Sir Leicester, and by an immense number of empty but 'inconsolable carriages'. From one of these, Mr Bucket observes his wife in the crowd, accompanying her lodger (Hortense). In Sir Leicester's town house, where Bucket receives one of innumerable anonymous letters accusing Lady Dedlock of the murder, he makes tactfully different bows, paying homage to Sir Leicester, gallantry to Volumnia, and recognition (as a man of the world) to the debilitated cousin. He announces that he has almost completed putting together his 'beautiful case' and he flatters 'Mercury' into confirming the precise time at which Lady Dedlock left the house, on the night of the murder, 'in a loose black mantle, with a deep fringe to it' (p. 816).

> Just how are we to classify Bucket? Like Turveydrop he finds 'gallantry' to women hard to resist, almost calling Volumnia 'my dear'. Like Tulkinghorn he relishes his sherry, and his access to the

great. Yet he appreciates his wife's society and her prowess in his sphere of detection. The reference to Mrs Bucket as 'a lady of natural detective genius, which if it had been improved by professional exercise, might have done great things' (p. 804) is one of many on the professional capacities of women.

XVII (CHAPTERS 54–6)

As Bucket reveals to Sir Leicester what Tulkinghorn had discovered of Lady Dedlock's past, Smallweed and the Chadbands arrive intent on blackmail. Dismissing them, Bucket arrests the murderess. Mrs Rouncewell and Guppy alarm Lady Dedlock into flight, at the very moment at which her innocence of the murder is established. Bucket sets out in pursuit

CHAPTER 54 SPRINGING A MINE

Relentless yet deferential, Bucket breaks to Sir Leicester the news that Tulkinghorn had discovered Lady Dedlock's premarital affair with Nemo, and that she visited Tulkinghorn's office on the night of the murder, dressed in a loose mantle with a deep fringe. He suspects that Tulkinghorn was about to reveal his discoveries, and was prevented by his death. As Sir Leicester lies in a state of shock, Grandfather Smallweed is borne in, followed by Mr and Mrs Chadband and Mrs Snagsby. The Smallweeds, having discovered Lady Dedlock's love letters hidden in Lady Jane's bed, had handed them over to Tulkinghorn and they want compensation. Mr Bucket produces the letters, and offers Smallweed £250. The Chadbands also want payment, for keeping the 'sinful secret' of Esther's birth. Mrs Snagsby is present because in her ceaseless search for evidence of Mr Snagsby's infidelity she brought Guppy's sleuthing activities to the attention of Tulkinghorn.

Having dismissed the blackmailing party, Mr Bucket announces that the murderess is in the house. He sends for Hortense, who spits out her contempt for Sir Leicester and his house. Bucket reveals how Mrs Bucket has not only watched Hortense writing anonymous letters, but also located the spot where the murder weapon was disposed of. The stricken Sir Leicester is left to muse on the fall of Lady Dedlock, who has been 'a stock of living tenderness and love' amid the strained formalities of his life, and whom he now sees 'almost to the exclusion of himself' (p. 838).

CHAPTER 55 FLIGHT

Mrs Bagnet has revealed to Mrs Rouncewell her detection of George's secret. Mother and son are reunited, in George's prison cell. Mrs Rouncewell pleads with an astonished Lady Dedlock to do what she can to clear George of suspicion, and leaves her with an anonymous letter, addressed to Mrs Rouncewell, accusing Lady Dedlock of the murder. A little later, Guppy arrives, to warn Lady Dedlock (when he gets to the point) that Smallweed and Mrs Chadband may have come into possession of the letters, and that they have been with Sir Leicester, this very morning. Facing arrest as a murderess or exposure as a fallen woman, Lady Dedlock feels pursued by the shadow of the man she had wished dead. She writes to Sir Leicester declaring her innocence of the murder, and her unworthiness of his generous devotion, and leaves.

CHAPTER 56 PURSUIT

Sir Leicester is found, having suffered a severe stroke. Mrs Rouncewell sends for Mr Bucket. Sir Leicester writes 'Full forgiveness. Find' (p. 859). Mr Bucket, understanding his new commission, investigates Lady Dedlock's room, selects Esther's handkerchief as its most eloquent talisman, and sets out in pursuit. From George he obtains Esther's address in Oxford Street. While he waits for Esther to dress, Bucket 'mounts a high tower in his mind' (p. 864) and looks out over a wintry landscape of dark figures, some wandering, some sheltering, some floating shapelessly on the tide.

> Both Sir Leicester and Lady Dedlock take on reversed roles at this stage of the novel. Sir Leicester is promoted from 'Sir Arrogant Numbskull' into a centre of sympathy, and the entire detective thrust of the narrative, hitherto devoted to pulling Lady Dedlock down, is now devoted to saving her.

XVIII (CHAPTERS 57–9)

While Esther and Bucket pursue Lady Dedlock, Sir Leicester keeps the fires burning to welcome her return

CHAPTER 57 ESTHER'S NARRATIVE [E]

Bucket pauses at a police station to distribute a description of Lady Dedlock, visits the city riverside, where something wet turns out not to be Lady Dedlock, and sets off to St Albans. Approaching Bleak House at daybreak Mr Bucket reveals how Mr Skimpole betrayed Jo to him for a five pound note. 'Whenever a person proclaims to you "In worldly matters I'm a child" … you have got that person's number, and it's Number One' (p. 875). At the brickmaker's house Jenny is absent, and Liz is prevented by her husband from saying anything. Jenny's husband admits that a lady did visit last night, but insists she went north, or rather that one went to 'Lunnun' and the other away from it. Bucket decides to take the road north. At first he seems on the track of an appropriately dressed woman, but the track is lost. He decides to return to London.

> Throughout this whole exciting chase the reader, who has now been trained in detection, is left to second-guess what Bucket is up to. Given that Esther is the soul of morality, her responses to Bucket are of considerable interest. Does she help us to decide about him?

CHAPTER 58 A WINTRY DAY AND NIGHT

Mrs Rouncewell fears that the end has come for the Dedlock family, and that Lady Dedlock will not return. Volumnia reveals to Sir Leicester that George Rouncewell has returned. George takes Sir Leicester in his arms, like a child. Sir Leicester recovers his speech enough to assert, before Volumnia and the Rouncewells, that he is on unaltered terms with Lady Dedlock, his affection undiminished, and no disposition in her favour revoked. His words, say the narrator, are 'honourable, manly, and true' (p. 895). The fires in Lady Dedlock's rooms are kept up in expectation of her return.

CHAPTER 58 continued

Sir Leicester's continued fineness to Lady Dedlock may provoke cynicism in modern readers; yet his forgiveness is the baronet's one positive action in the novel. It seems that in one respect, at least, Dickens can admire aristocratic values. Sir Leicester's loyalty seems calculated to challenge the narrow, bourgeois moralism Dickens would have attributed to almost all his readers.

CHAPTER 59 ESTHER'S NARRATIVE [E]

Esther and Bucket arrive in Islington, the former still worried that they are getting further and further from her mother. To Bucket, Esther is 'a pattern'; she is 'as mild as she's game, and as game as she's mild', in short 'a Queen' (p. 902). From Chancery Lane, where they meet Woodcourt, they go to Mr Snagsby's. Esther meets for the first time 'a scared sorrowful-looking little man' (p. 906) and very severe woman who has scared Guster into one of her fits. While Woodcourt attempts to bring Guster out of her fit, so she will release a paper she holds (a letter Lady Dedlock has written to Esther during her flight), Bucket puts Mrs Snagsby right about Mr Snagsby and various ladies. With 'a soul too large for your body … and chafing it' (p. 908), he tells her flatteringly, Mrs Snagsby has shut her eyes '(and sparklers too)' and run her delicate-formed head against a wall.

When Guster tells them Lady Dedlock was seeking a pauper's graveyard with an archway, Bucket leads Esther to the place, where she thinks she sees Jenny, 'the mother of the dead child'. At first she cannot grasp that it is her mother.

Esther's diminishing intuition at this stage of the novel is a problem. She has failed to guess Ada's marriage, though Jarndyce does; now she fails to see what Bucket and the reader have grasped throughout the chapter. The style of the two dramatic chapters narrating Bucket's pursuit is heightened by Esther's innocence, but is there any further significance in her attribution of quicker intuition to two males? Why does Lady Dedlock die? Is she a scapegoat?

XIX & XX (CHAPTERS 60–7)

Esther becomes the mistress of Bleak House; the case of Jarndyce and Jarndyce is resolved by the discovery of a will among Krook's papers; George is reunited with his brother, and a grey cloak and umbrella become a regular sight at Chesney Wold; Richard 'begins the world' and Jarndyce takes Ada and her child under his wing

CHAPTER 60 PERSPECTIVE [E]

Allan Woodcourt is to become a medical attendant to the poor in the Yorkshire dales. Miss Flite is alarmed by Richard's connection with the dangerous Vholes, but to honour Richard's constant attendance at court has made him her executor. Vholes remarks that Richard's marriage, given the state of his affairs, is ill-advised. Ada, even more the 'angel in the house', is determined never to show Richard 'that I grieved for what he did' (p. 928). She is expecting a child, but fears Richard may not live to see it.

> Ada's fears are more than confirmed in Miss Flite's chilling remarks on Richard as 'Gridley's successor' and on the fact that she has added 'The Wards in Jarndyce' to her caged collection along with 'Hope, Joy, Youth, Despair … Precedent, Jargon, Gammon and Spinach' (p. 922). Moreover, Richard's declining health seems not unconnected to Vholes having 'something of the Vampire in him' (p. 924).

CHAPTER 61 A DISCOVERY [E]

Esher gets Skimpole to promise not to go near Richard. She also accuses him bluntly of betraying Jarndyce's confidence for a bribe. She tells us that, years later, in his autobiography, Skimpole called Jarndyce 'the Incarnation of Selfishness' (p. 935). Woodcourt escorts Esther home from Richard's, and reveals – but 'O, too late' – that what she had thought was pity is still love. She declares herself proud to have won his love, but still happy in her engagement to 'the best of human beings' (p. 939).

Incrementally the reader is being manipulated into desiring that Esther should recognise, and act on, the difference between feeling gratitude and being in love.

CHAPTER 62 ANOTHER DISCOVERY [E]

Esther goes to sleep repeating the words of 'the letter', which she knows by heart. She and Jarndyce agree that she will become the mistress of Bleak House in a month. Mr Smallweed arrives, having found a will in the case, and Bucket negotiates its release to Jarndyce in return for a reward relative to its value. Mr Kenge reveals that the will advances Richard's and Ada's interests.

The chapter is notable both for sustaining two illusions – that Esther will marry Jarndyce, and that there might be such a thing as an end to Jarndyce and Jarndyce. It also gives one of the best examples of a repeated phenomenon, the effect of introducing a character from one narrative into another: here Esther gets her first glimpse of Grandfather Smallweed. Does he appear more human?

CHAPTER 63 STEEL AND IRON

George visits the iron country, where he finds his brother's name everywhere. Amid a great perplexity of iron, fireworks of it bubbling in its youth, and mountains of it broken up and rusty in its age, he finds his brother. He is invited to a farewell party for Rosa, who is going to Germany to finish her education. But he resists the invitation to join his brother's enterprise, preferring to stay with Sir Leicester's 'household brigade'. Before riding back to 'the green country' he sends to Esther the letter he had made available to Tulkinghorn. In this letter Hawdon asked George to deliver another letter to 'a young and beautiful lady, then unmarried in England' (p. 958).

Dickens does not show Rouncewell's enterprise in a very positive light, as the salvation of England. Rouncewell is clearly the man of the future, yet his rusty iron-yard seems as disorderly and as prone to rot as every other part of England.

It is noteworthy that George reminds the reader (and Esther) of Nemo's love-letters to Esther's mother, prior to her marriage to Sir

Leicester, while Esther is preparing to make a similar mistake by marrying Jarndyce instead of Woodcourt. This is the only preparation Dickens makes for what happens in the next chapter.

Germany Dickens's weekly *Household Words* regularly reported on the superiority of German society in such matters as poor relief and universal education

CHAPTER 64 ESTHER'S NARRATIVE [E]

While preparing a trousseau to please Jarndyce's taste, Esther is summoned to Yorkshire where Allan's new home has been prepared by Jarndyce to match Esther's taste. Its name is Bleak House. 'Genially, like the ripening weather', Jarndyce explains how soon he had realised the love between Esther and Woodcourt. As he would not allow Esther to be 'admitted on sufferance into the line of Morgan ap Kerrig' he had told Mrs Woodcourt that he knew how Esther would 'sacrifice her love to a sense of duty and affection, and will sacrifice it so completely, so entirely, so religiously, that you should never suspect it, though you watched her night and day' (p. 965). He gave his consent to Allan speaking to her of his love; and Allan reported back. In what is almost an informal wedding ceremony, in the garden of Bleak House (away from the corruptions of formal religion?) Jarndyce, more fatherly than ever, 'gives Esther away'. When Guppy later renews his proposal, Jarndyce rejects it on her behalf. Mrs Guppy furiously demands that Jarndyce leave his own house!

> The fact that Jarndyce is absolutely right about Esther's feelings cannot, for the modern reader, excuse the astonishing way in which he hands her over to Allan without asking her. In the brilliant BBC production, surprisingly faithful in every other respect, the producers bottled out and wrote a scene in which Jarndyce and Esther have a grown-up conversation and agree to set aside their engagement. Are we, perhaps, *meant* to feel aggrieved on Esther's behalf, and to see how in the Chancery world, even Jarndyce treats people – however benignly – as objects? On the other hand, in rejecting Guppy, Jarndyce is clearly speaking on Esther's behalf, in his proper role as her guardian, and with her entire consent.

CHAPTER 65 BEGINNING OF THE WORLD [E]

The case of Jarndyce and Jarndyce is over, not because the will has been proved, but because the entire estate has been consumed in costs. Mr Kenge speaks of how the flower of the Bar and the mature autumnal fruits of the Woolsack have been lavished upon the suit. Mr Vholes gives Esther a devouring look and emits 'one gasp as if he had swallowed the last morsel of his client' (p. 976). Richard, with one parting sob, begins 'The world that sets this right' (p. 979), and Miss Flite gives her birds their liberty.

> When Jarndyce, at Richard's deathbed, puts a lock of Ada's hair to his lips, is this meant to remind us of Krook? Is anyone entirely free of selfishness?

CHAPTER 66 DOWN IN LINCOLNSHIRE

Lady Dedlock (scandalising the fashionable intelligence) lies in the mausoleum at Chesney Wold, a place of gathering darkness and vacancy, where most of the house is now shut up, and the light of the drawing-room 'seems gradually contracting and dwindling until it shall be no more' (p. 983). Mr Boythorn keeps up the contest over rights of way, but only to humour Sir Leicester. Phil Squod works in the stables. George accompanies his mother to church, and they are visited by the Bagnets. Volumnia reads to Sir Leicester, in a state of boredom relieved only by her mention in his will.

> The paragraph of **anaphora** (p. 984), addressed to Volumnia, the tuckered sylph, is a final stylistic flourish, reminding of the **satirical** malice this narrative has mostly abandoned. Contrasted with the gambolling Bagnet daughters, Volumnia is compared to the chandeliers with their 'disappointing knobs where no drops are' (p. 984). In a startling piece of sexual **symbolism** she shares the sterility of this place of 'unused passages' (p. 985).

CHAPTER 67 THE CLOSE OF ESTHER'S NARRATIVE [E]

Now married for seven years, Esther concludes her narrative. Ada and Richard's child – 'my Richard', says Esther – resume life at the old Bleak House with their 'guardian'. Charley has married a prosperous miller, where her little brother is apprenticed, and Emma, her sister, is Esther's new maid. Caddy drives her own carriage, and runs the business as her husband is lame, and does her best to be a mother to her deaf mute child. Mrs Jellyby has tired of Africa and gone in for women's rights. Jarndyce remains 'a superior being'. Esther is rich in the praises her husband earns from the poor. Her final sentence implies the restoration of 'my old looks – such as they were'.

> The two endings, one sombre but brightened by the Bagnet girls, the other bright but darkened by Caddy's suffering daughter, are conventional enough. The devotion of the final page to the matter of Esther's looks – and whether she is recovering them – is also fairly conventional. Yet Allan's teasing is interesting. When Esther refers to her vanished looks, he reminds her to add 'such as they were'. The passage seems designed to suggest that Esther has made the passage from self-deprecation to self-esteem.

> You may need to read this chapter several times before noticing that Esther has two daughters (they are mentioned as an afterthought but not named). The fact that she ignores her own children and names 'my Richard' repeatedly, creates a new note of ambiguity. Could Esther be a neglectful parent? Or is it that she is not quite reconciled to thinking of herself as a mother? Dickens specialised in endings that combine clarity about the fates of all the minor characters, while leaving the central one a little mysterious, but as far as I know, this final mystery has never been noticed by critics.

PART THREE

CRITICAL APPROACHES

THEMES

Dickens was a journalist as well as a novelist. He started professional life as a reporter on the *Morning News*, and edited two popular weeklies, first *Household Words* – which started publication in 1850, the year before he began serialising *Bleak House* – and later *All the Year Round*. Not surprisingly, then, his work has a sharp flavour of topicality. It is characteristic of his imagination to take materials from contemporary documents and convert them into fiction. Thus, *Household Words* (January 1850) carried the following transcript of a testimony by a boy of fourteen called George Ruby:

> *Alderman:* Do you know what an oath is?
> *Boy:* No.
> *Alderman:* Can you read?
> *Boy:* No.
> *Alderman:* Do you ever say your prayers?
> *Boy:* No, never.
> *Alderman:* Do you know what prayers are?
> *Boy:* No.
> *Alderman:* Do you know what God is?
> *Boy:* No.
> *Alderman:* Do you know what the devil is?
> *Boy:* I've heard of the devil, but I don't know him.
> *Alderman:* What do you know?
> *Boy:* I knows how to sweep the crossings.
> (quoted in Humphry House, *The Dickens World*, OUP 1960, pp. 32–3)

In *Bleak House* Dickens translates this passage into two memorable moments. The first is in Chapter 11 (p. 177) where the Coroner interrogates Jo to see whether his evidence can be accepted (here the dialogue is converted into summary **reportage**, giving Jo's answers to implied questions). The second is the attempt of Allan Woodcourt to teach him the Lord's Prayer on his deathbed (Chapter 47, pp. 733–4).

Household Words was designed to inform the public about issues of the moment. It published investigative journalism on such matters as industrial accidents, the living conditions of the poor, women's property rights and education. Its 'mission' (**ironically**, in view of what is said about people with missions in *Bleak House*, Dickens certainly had a mission) was to 'fight for tolerance and the progress of human welfare, and give no quarter to chicanery and oppression' (Edgar Johnson, *Charles Dickens: His Tragedy and Triumph*, 1953, Vol. 2, p. 703). The depiction of an intolerant world, in which the strong oppress the weak, there is much chicanery and no sign whatever of appropriate welfare for such as Jo, Jenny and Guster, might be said to be what *Bleak House*, also, is about. The novel is part of Dickens's campaign against the national complacency expressed in the Great Exhibition of 1851, at which event the then Archbishop of Canterbury – sounding not unlike a grander Reverend Chadband – expressed thanks that there is in England neither violence nor destruction, but 'peace within our walls and plenteousness within our palaces' (quoted from John Lucas, *Charles Dickens: the Major Novels*, Penguin, 1992, p. 72).

THE LAW

Despite Dickens's choice of the Court of Chancery as his central **symbol** and most obvious '**theme**', the minutiae of legal practice (what solicitors and barristers and the Lord Chancellor actually do and how they do it) are less relevant than the deeper idea of what the Court of Chancery symbolises; namely, that people are born into disputes over rights and property, and vainly spend their lives seeking equity.

The law, of course, provides work for a whole tribe of solicitors, barristers, law stationers, law writers, debt collectors and bailiffs who all, therefore, have an interest in 'the system'. As embodied in Tulkinghorn, the system protects the strong and bullies the weak, and it reaches out through its agents (Inspector Bucket and Grandfather Smallweed are both essentially agents of Tulkinghorn) to oppress and pursue whoever might in any way threaten the stability of the system, or of patrimony – whether Jo the crossing sweeper, or Gridley the suitor, or Lady Dedlock herself.

In William Blake's poem, 'London', everyone and every thing is 'chartered': that is, defined and delimited by documents. The speaker of Blake's poem laments the 'mind-forged manacles' which can be seen in every face and heard in every voice, as 'marks of weakness, marks of woe'. Commercial manacles connect the sweep, the soldier, the harlot and the newborn infant as blighted victims of a system of exploitation upheld by church and state. In Dickens's opening paragraphs blank legalism is the essence of London: 'London. Michaelmas term lately over, and the Lord Chancellor sitting in Lincoln's Inn Hall ... Fog everywhere'. These associations imply a system of negations. The law, like fog, covers everyone and everything in a blanket of mystery and inertia. But the system only seems random and inert. In reality, once you understand that 'the one great principle of the English law is to make business for itself' (p. 621), for instance by converting land and property into income for lawyers, it all makes perfect sense. Chancery, which draws in hopeless suitors from Shropshire and Hertfordshire alike, turning entire London streets into 'the property of costs', also reaches out to grasp 'decaying houses and blighted lands in every shire' and to entangle acres of land in meshes of sheepskin. It spreads like infection; and can therefore be treated as a co-symbol with typhus and cholera, which, as it happens, thrive on the poverty and dereliction Chancery creates.

So in *Bleak House*, as several critics have recognised, the Court of Chancery is

- an actual abuse Dickens wants reformed
- a symbol of what is wrong with the whole social system and of the laws (in a more general sense) by which we live
- the basis of an **allegory** of man's living 'in expectation of a judgement', which will be associated in some sense with the fires of apocalypse
- a symptom of human selfishness and combativeness

The legal case which provides the novel with its major plot, 'Jarndyce and Jarndyce', is based upon a real case which had begun in 1834, involved up to forty lawyers, and incurred costs of £70,000 by the time Dickens was writing. Gridley's story is based on another factual case. Another case known to Dickens had begun in 1798 and was still unsettled in 1851. In 1851, not surprisingly, the newspapers published angry denunciations of the Court of Chancery and its wasteful practices. John Butt and Kathleen

Tillotson, in 'The Topicality of Bleak House' (1957) give wonderfully **satirical** examples from *The Times*:

> To ... Englishmen the Court of Chancery is a name of terror, a devouring gulf, a den whence no footsteps return. Ask why such a family was ruined, why the representatives of a wealthy man are wanderers over the face of the earth, why the butlers, and housekeepers, and gardeners of the kindest masters in the world, in spite of ample legacies in his will are rotting on parish pay, why the best house in the street is falling to decay, its windows all broken, and its very doors disappearing, why such a one drowned himself, and another is disgraced – you are as likely as not to hear that a Chancery suit is at the bottom of it.
>
> Thirty-six years are something in the life of a man, of a nation, of a dynasty, or even of a planet, but in the history of a chancery suit they are a brief interval ... We leave our suits to our children ... The little plaintiffs and defendants grow up for the benefit of Chancery; and she adopts them as naturally as they succeed to us.
> (quoted in A.E. Dyson, ed., *Dickens: Bleak House*, Macmillan, 1969, pp. 114, 115)

These editorials, with their brilliant **imagery** and rhythmic prose, might be quotations from the novel, and Richard and Ada are clearly fictional counterparts of these adopted plaintiffs, just as Jo is a fictional George Ruby. Journalism was a far more literary craft in Dickens's day than in our own, and such quotations help to remind one that what sometimes seems Dickens's exaggerated **rhetoric** actually creates a bridge to the 'real' world of his time.

SANITATION & DISEASE

One of Dickens's charges against Chancery is that much urban blight can be traced to its proceedings, and the most decayed areas of London and other great cities were of course plagued by outbreaks of cholera and typhus. As Humphry House says, when Dickens wrote *Bleak House*, people 'were ... dying of litigation and of cholera' (*The Dickens World*, p. 33). The press complained about the impossibility of eradicating disease without decent sanitation, decent housing and fresh water. This was the era of such great investigative documents as Sir Edwin Chadwick's *Inquiry into the Sanitary Condition of the Labouring Population of Great Britain* (1842), Friedrich Engels, *The Condition of the Working Class in England in 1844*, and less well known documents such as John

Simon's *Report on the Sanitary Condition of the City* (1850) – a review of which is included in A. E. Dyson's casebook on *Bleak House*. Charles Kingsley, the Christian Socialist novelist, reviewing Simon in the *North British Review* (1851), six months before Dickens started writing *Bleak House*, demanded the immediate establishment of a publicly owned water supply, because:

> Unless some practical proof is given to the suffering masses who inhabit our courts and alleys … that a constitutional government can secure more palpable benefits to the many than a tyranny; unless human beings [cease to be] sacrificed to a proposition in a yet infant and tentative science [economics], – we must expect to see, in the course of events, a revulsion in favour of despotism …
> (*North British Review*, May 1851, p. 252)

Dickens doesn't pose directly the question of revolution in *Bleak House*. Perhaps he doesn't need to. His readers knew very well the equation: clean water = effective government. Thomas Carlyle's great historical work on the *History of the French Revolution* (1837) described that revolution not as a once-for-all historical event but as an ongoing process which might yet (and deservedly) reach England: 1848 was a year of revolutions throughout Europe and such 'spontaneous combustion' seemed possible in England. Dickens's readers knew that to present a picture of decaying slums, fever-houses and streams of pollution, alongside **satire** of the ineffectual leadership of Boodle, Coodle, Doodle and Foodle was to raise, implicitly, the question Thomas Carlyle asked at the end of *Sartor Resartus* (1833):

> Would Destiny offer Mankind that after say two centuries of convulsion and conflagration … the fire-creation should be accomplished, and we to find ourselves again in a Living Society … were it not perhaps *prudent* in mankind to strike the bargain?

Bleak House is full of victims of fever, whether cholera, typhus or smallpox, and these are treated not as a natural disaster but as the inevitable result of living conditions which are the direct responsibility of those who claim to govern. Guster, Jo, Esther are all victims – and by implication, Esther is afflicted by pollution carried from the pauper graveyard where Nemo is buried or from that blighted Chancery property, Tom-all-Alone's. Dickens's lack of faith in governmental action comes out in the fact that nobody in the novel even mentions sanitary reform, and the only persons attempting to do anything to provide relief for the poor are the doctor, Allan Woodcourt and the heroine, Esther.

CONSTITUTIONAL DEADLOCK

The failure of Parliament to take practical steps to improve the lot of the people in this or in any respect is a further related theme. In *Hard Times* MPs are referred to as the 'national dustmen' (for ever throwing dust in each other's eyes), and the most corrupt or misguided characters in *Hard Times*, *Our Mutual Friend*, and *Little Dorrit* are MPs. In *Bleak House* they are presented as inbred, financially corrupt, useless and interchangeable. The **satire** on politicians named Boodle, Coodle, Doodle and Foodle, in Chapters 12 and 40, is based on an actual moment in 1851 when for two weeks there was no government because none of the two or three 'people to speak of' was available to head it. In Chapter 16 their unfitness to govern is expressly linked to Tom-all-Alone's, where swarms of misery and foul existence come and go 'carrying fever and sowing more evil … than Lord Coodle, and Sir Thomas Doodle, and the Duke of Foodle, and all the fine gentlemen in office, down to Zoodle, shall set right in five hundred years – though born expressly to do it' (p. 257).

The assumption of the Dedlock family that the fate of the country is necessarily and eternally bound up with the Dedlock interest is subjected to considerable satire, even though Dickens's portrait of Sir Leicester himself becomes increasingly sympathetic. This ambivalence, which is felt throughout the novel, expresses Dickens's own. France had provided a discouraging example of what revolution can lead to and Dickens seems poised between a desire to sweep away all traces of what the Dedlocks represent – which is, not to put too fine a point on it, as Mr Snagsby would say, social deadlock and decay – and a poignant recognition that mob rule would sweep away something intrinsically valuable. Sir Leicester's apprehension (because Mr Rouncewell and his son have opposed the Dedlock interests in the elections) that 'the floodgates of society are burst open, and the waters have – a – obliterated the landmarks of the framework of the cohesion by which things are held together' (p. 648) is wonderfully comic, but he is himself, though a buffoon, a very *decent* buffoon.

So Chesney Wold, to the exasperation of critics, is confusingly depicted both as part of the *disease* and as part of the *antidote*. There *is* something between the Rouncewells and the Dedlocks which is not reducible to what Carlyle called the 'cash nexus' and one brother's devoted service (like his mother's) is treated with as much respect as the other brother's dignified distance. Rosa's rescue from Chesney Wold by young Watt and his father is, of course, a liberation. Yet the fact that at the end of the novel the country seat is graced by visits by 'a grey cloak and umbrella' seems to constitute a kind of approval. Dickens's revolutionary, apocalyptic leanings (derived from Carlyle's desire for a 'fire-creation' of a new and living society) are tempered by a sense that all we have to keep us human is love, compassion, a few beatitudes and a sense – as in Matthew Arnold's 'Dover Beach' – that we must 'be true to one another'. The antidote to social ills may be revolution; but it is more likely to be love.

THE WOMAN QUESTION

(See also Background.)

One of the floodgates that seemed to be opening rather rapidly in 1851 – with nobody knew what consequences – related to the proper sphere of women. *Bleak House* was published at a time of unprecedented agitation on 'the woman question' and Dickens's dual narrative, shared with an illegitimate young woman, who **symbolises** woman's exclusion from legal existence, is a major imaginative response to that major issue. It may even imply that social progress depends upon a fusion, an androgynous fusion, of male and female mindsets. Esther herself, though by our standards she may seem excessively deferential to men, and confined to the domestic sphere, is very alert to the position of women. She has 'a very noticing way', as she tells us in her first chapter, and she especially notices such things as Turveydrop's 'disagreeable gallantry', Guppy's stalking, the physical and emotional abuse of wives, and Caddy Jellyby's 'new woman' propensities – taking over her husband's and father-in-law's business. Mrs Jellyby and Mrs Pardiggle are criticised for using their formidable powers unwisely, but the novel's insistent ridicule of male assumptions of superiority makes central for the first time in Dickens's work a theme he will make his own in the classic brother/sister pairings of *Hard Times* and *Our Mutual Friend*.

Within a few pages of the third-person narrative there are these two parallel scenes. The first is between Mr Bagnet, George and Mrs Bagnet (p. 443):

> 'You act according to my opinion?'
>
> 'I shall be guided,' replies George, 'entirely by it.'
>
> 'Old girl,' says Mr Bagnet, 'give him my opinion. You know it. Tell him what it is.'

The second is between Lady Dedlock, Sir Leicester and the Ironmaster (p. 452):

> 'Am I to understand, sir,' says Sir Leicester, 'and is my Lady to understand;' he brings her in thus specially, first as a point of gallantry, and next as a point of prudence, having great reliance on her sense; '... that you consider this young woman [Rosa] too good for Chesney Wold ...?'
>
> 'Certainly not, Sir Leicester.'
>
> 'I am glad to hear it.' Sir Leicester very lofty indeed.
>
> 'Pray, Mr Rouncewell,' says my Lady, warning Sir Leicester off with the slightest gesture of her pretty hand, as if he were a fly, 'explain to me what you mean.'

Proper male deference to genuine female superiority is clearly analogous in the two scenes.

Part of the feminist case has to do with brutality to women, dramatised in the novel's concern with domestic violence (and Bucket's evident familiarity with it), and with the more subtle exploitation of Mrs Turveydrop and Mrs Skimpole by their husbands. Mrs Jellyby and Mrs Pardiggle, too, treat their husbands and children as objects, and are rebuked for doing so. But the powerful figures of Mrs Bagnet and Lady Dedlock are clearly admired (by the male **narrator**) for managing their husbands, necessarily and tactfully, since they are evidently much brighter than their partners.

SELFISHNESS, EXPLOITATION, REIFICATION, APPROPRIATION

Obvious themes of the novel are selfishness and greed. One function of the range of unselfish characters, such as Mrs Blinder, Esther, Jarndyce,

George, the Bagnets, is to bring out, by contrast, how in the bad characters selfishness is endemic and raised to a very high pitch indeed. In the Chancery world everyone seems to be caught up in a web of acquisition and exploitation, which is most vividly caught in the Smallweed family, who make it a matter of principle to exploit Charley, George, Jobling, or anyone on whom they can acquire some leverage. In *Bleak House* human life seems a matter of sizing up people for what can be found out about them, and consequently got out of them. Parasitism, embodied in the Hon. Bob Stables or Turveydrop, Skimpole, or Richard, seems ubiquitous. In the case of Vholes, explicitly, and Krook and Smallweed implicitly, it is figured as vampirism.

PHILANTHROPY

Another major topical theme is organised charity. In 1841 the Exeter Hall Missionary Society had despatched a particularly disastrous expedition to the Niger to abolish slavery and improve agriculture. In Mrs Jellyby Dickens **satirises** the folly and the hypocrisy of remote and impracticable charitable activities, especially those which ignore the desperate plight of the English poor, and seek to export civilisation from the dark heart of 'this boastful island'. If you really want to explore the heart of darkness, *Bleak House* suggests, find a policeman, or a doctor, to guide you into the fever houses of Tom-all-Alone's – where life, while it lasts, is brutal, bestial and verminous. As John Lucas points out, *Bleak House* can be seen as an attempt to enlighten the decent middle class (**symbolised** in the inoffensive, innocent, bewildered Mr Snagsby?) about what horrors lay around them, just out of sight, ignored and imaginatively unknown.

Like Gaskell's more circumstantial but also more idealised account of Manchester working-class life (Mrs Gaskell's working-class figures in *Mary Barton* are unvaryingly kind, gentle and considerate), *Bleak House* attempts to convert the teeming data of inquiries and reports into working-class life, into imaginatively grasped reality. Gaskell had led the middle-class reader into the reality of working-class poverty, starvation, disease and death. Dickens exposes the same reader to a darker sense of ignorance, brutality, drunkenness and violence, and presents these as symptoms of a diseased system in which the official means of making things better – Parliament, the law and organised religion – are simply making things worse.

Apart from Esther, the likeliest points of contact between the poor and the respectable world are a policeman (who will assume that any half-crown found on a crossing-sweeper is stolen) or a Mrs Pardiggle. These, between them, represent a vast middle-class apparatus engaged in condescension, intrusion, surveillance and control. One of the most memorable speeches in the novel is that of the brickmaker greeting that appallingly insensitive agent of middle-class virtue, Mrs Pardiggle:

> 'Have I read the little book wot you left? No, I an't read the little book wot you left. There an't nobody here as knows how to read it; and if there wos, it wouldn't be suitable to me. It's a book fit for a babby, and I'm not a babby ... How have I been conducting of myself? Why, I've been drunk for three days; and I'd a been drunk four, if I'd a had the money ... And how did my wife get that black eye? Why, I giv' it her; and if she says I didn't, she's a Lie!' (p. 132)

Dickens is capable of exaggeration and of sentimentality and of fantasy, but this speech shows him capable of something close to naturalism: the brickmaker's pugnaciousness may be part of his general brutishness, but we are likely to enjoy it because it exposes the irrelevance and the class insolence of Mrs Pardiggle. The practical, sensitive, compassionate caring practised by Esther or Ada, or of Mr Jarndyce and Trooper George, of Jenny and her friend, is quite another matter.

DANDYISM, PUSEYISM, AESTHETICISM, ARISTOCRACY

One function of Mrs Pardiggle is to **satirise** one aspect of what Dickens calls 'Dandyism', that is, a Dandyism in Religion that wants to set the clock back several hundred years. She is a 'Puseyite', associated with high church practices, such as the establishment of Anglican sisterhoods on Catholic models. Since almost everything in this novel seems to signify by analogy with something else, it is easy to see that Mrs Pardiggle's religious Dandyism is analogous to Turveydrop's literal Dandyism, in modelling his deportment on the Prince Regent, the vacuous speaking styles of the Reverend Chadband or Conversation Kenge, the heartless aestheticism of Skimpole (who represents among other things, the 'art for art's sake' tendency that Dickens deplored), the aristocratic style of Sir

Leicester, and, of course, the whole backward looking, ineffectual world of Parliament and Chancery.

SHADOWING & DETECTION: INTERPRETING SIGNS

In J. Hillis Miller's famous argument (once available as the introduction to the Penguin edition; now the opening essay in Jeremy Tambling's New Casebook; see Critical History) the novel is essentially about language: about naming, reading signs, interpreting. The characters are constantly poring over signs and documents and seeking to decipher meanings and identities. The reader is decoyed into the game of detection in which almost all the characters are engaged, and may even feel frustrated by the way the deaths of Nemo, and Krook, and Tulkinghorn frustrate the early completion of the ostensible plot, which is the unmasking of Lady Dedlock. As Miller points out, we are all implicated in the moral quagmire of the novel by allowing ourselves to accuse the wrong character of the murder of Tulkinghorn: and it is the innocent George and the official Bucket who invite us to do so.

Both narrators ask leading questions of us, invite us to add two and two and make five, and lay a trail of clues. The impersonal narrator's famous question – 'What connection can there be, between the place in Lincolnshire and the whereabouts of Jo the outlaw with the broom?' (in Chapter 16) – is **rhetorical** at first, though slowly answered: the connection is that by seeking out the 'outlaw' to retrace the last days of her former lover, Lady Dedlock brings down that Norman House. Dickens lays some false clues, of course, so that the reader is likely to be as mistaken as Mrs Snagsby. But he also plants quite remarkably subtle linguistic clues – which seem to be placed there to be enjoyed only on a second or third reading – for instance when Nemo is described as having left no more track than a deserted infant (p. 196) or when Esther sees Lady Dedlock and says 'I knew the beautiful face quite well' (p. 304).

TECHNIQUE

THE DUAL NARRATIVE

Like other multiple narratives, Emily Brontë's *Wuthering Heights* (1847) and Wilkie Collins's *The Moonstone* (1868), this novel invites the reader to become engaged in a process of judgement, while making that process more difficult by the very manner in which it is told. It is the first novel to be narrated by interleaving, throughout its length, two deeply contrasting narratives, each with its own style, its own experience, and its own values. It is also, surprisingly, the first English novel in which a male novelist assumes the guise (in part) of a woman writer.

Its two narratives employ contrasts of person, gender, tone, tense and values. First we have an impersonal narration, in the historic present, by an omniscient observer, whose concern is with the proceedings of Chancery and the downfall of the Dedlocks. It covers an immense social and geographic range, and is capable of microscopic close-up in which even the animal tissues of legal parchments become vividly present, or of panoramic vistas in which the entire constitutional fabric is reduced to absurdity and entire classes of people reduced to robots. It is angry, pessimistic, indignant, controlled, and capable of levelling itself at the sovereign herself on equal terms, hectoring her and all her right reverends and wrong reverends for taking too little heed of those who are 'dying thus around us everyday'. It is also, without a doubt, male: public, analytical, not to be taken in by appearances, knowing, experienced, worldly.

Secondly, we have the autobiographical narrative of Esther which concerns her search for an identity, and her story (probably more important to her than to us) of Ada and Richard – Jarndyce's wards – 'beginning the world'. Its tone is generally self-deprecating, appreciative, tender, although she can offer penetrating and correct judgements on characters when she wants to. Although the work of a mature married woman, this information is withheld until the end: the narrative has all the diffidence of an inexperienced, unworldly, repressed, illegitimate young woman thoroughly dependent on others for her 'progress' from stigma to acceptance and unable to see herself (without embarrassment) as the centre of her own story until its closing paragraph. It is also, inescapably, female: as female as Dickens could make it. Yet it comes to confirm, from its own point of view, the other narrator's grim view of

Chancery: in fact, she takes over this theme almost entirely from the other narrator once 'he' has initiated it.

That is, the narratives do not merely lead to the same complex denouements: the parentage of Esther, the consumption of Jarndyce and Jarndyce in its own costs, the tragedy of the Dedlocks, and the uniting of Mrs Rouncewell with her long lost son. They also enrich each other by giving double perspectives on events. There is a sort of arch created by the impersonal narrative leaning towards sympathetic identification, and the personal one learning the necessity of judgement. You could see this as a deliberate stylistic marriage of a male and female perspective, in which each learns from the other. The male narrative learns empathy and exudes sentiment – especially in treating the Bagnets and the Rouncewells – while the female narrative learns judgement and even toughness of mind. At the same time the two narrators leave the novel suspended between one narrative's sense of universal entropy and the other's qualified optimism.

Critics disagree quite violently, by the way, about whether, in the end, the narratives coalesce into one moral vision, or remain divided so as to imply the ultimate impossibility of reaching one view of the world. Equally, of course, critics divide over Esther herself. To some she is a blight and a bore, a major tactical mistake on Dickens's part. To some she is valuable mainly because her steady, plodding, static vision gives us a rest from the other narrator's mercurial wit and savage **irony**. To others, she is literature's most brilliant study of the psychology of illegitimacy; and to yet others, a fascinating attempt by a male narrator to explore the repressions brought about in a young woman by a patriarchal society. Recent criticism, especially that of Suzanne Graver and Brenda Ayres, has come to focus on the fascination of watching a male novelist, who liked the notion of separate spheres for male and female activity, exploring the self-divisions within a young woman trying to accommodate herself to that vision.

SERIALISATION: PLUSES & MINUSES

One obvious technical aspect of the novel is that it was written for serial publication. Among the effects of this are that the writer has to give the customer a sense of something fully realised in each episode. That may be why *Bleak House*, as W. J. Harvey complained, sometimes tends 'to exploit to the full the possibilities of any particular scene, situation or action without too much regard for the relevance of such local intensities to the total work of art' (Casebook, p. 224). Put more positively, this accounts for the elaboration of minor characters and minor episodes in a way that can become wearisome to the reader of the final, unitary novel.

Another effect of serialisation, especially given the number of characters involved, and the great intervals that may separate their appearances, is that Dickens developed a way of giving his characters a catch phrase (Jarndyce's 'floored again'), a manner of speech (in Snagsby's 'my li-ttle woman', or Hortense's 'I des-pise you' the placing of the hyphen distinguishes between English and foreign intonation very well), or some other identifying tag, such as Bucket consulting his forefinger. It may seem simple as a technique, but there are nineteenth-century novelists in whose novels it is immensely difficult to remember who is who, and Dickens's technique was borrowed gratefully by such a different writer as Joseph Conrad.

Occasionally, also, one wonders whether Dickens's own sense of what he wants to do with his characters changes in the course of composition. Compare the different impressions made by Sir Leicester at different stages in the novel; or the change from comic treatment of Mr Jarndyce (all 'east wind' and 'floored again') to portrayal of him as an urbane and courteous gentleman; or the slight inconsistency in accounts of Esther's birth (did she die 'in the first hours of her life' [p. 469], or was it that she 'never ... breathed' [p. 583]?); or the gradual darkening of Skimpole. These may be seen as troubling inconsistencies; or as aspects of a novel that evolves organically, as Dickens revises his first intentions in the course of composition. In some novels, such as *Martin Chuzzlewit*, he even made changes in response to public feedback.

SATIRE, IRONY, HUMOUR, COMEDY

At least two writers on Dickens have made the (to me) astonishing claim that it is hard to find any humour in *Bleak House*. Certainly, the book is lacking in the pure comic spirit of celebration, except perhaps in such scenes as Mrs Bagnet's birthday party. And the humorous depictions can be of a somewhat macabre or grotesque kind, as they are also in *Our*

Mutual Friend and *Great Expectations*. But it would be a strange reader who could read aloud Mrs Piper's evidence at the Inquest, or Guppy's proposal of marriage, or Esther's treatment of the astonishing Mrs Guppy, or her impressions of Mrs Pardiggle and her ferociously discontented children, or of Mr Turveydrop, or Mrs Bagnet's management of Mr Bagnet, or Mrs Snagsby's delusions concerning Mr Snagsby, or the opinions of the 'debilitated cousin', or Sir Leicester's apoplectic responses to Mr Rouncewell and his activities, without laughing aloud.

Take Mrs Snagsby's nose for instance: only a great comic writer would have the timing and the audacity to describe Mrs Snagsby as having 'a sharp nose like a sharp Autumn evening, inclining to be frosty towards the end' (p. 135). The sentence is just long enough to give one time, at the comma, to meditate the surreal **simile** (how can a nose be like an evening?) before its import is revealed in a sort of quadruple pun on 'end' (of nose, evening, year, and sentence). On the same page the sanguine Cock at Cook's corner is introduced, 'whose ideas of daylight it would be curious to ascertain, since he knows from his personal observation next to nothing about it.' Here the human register ('ideas', 'personal observation') provides the gentle, mellow humour, which will be augmented at each reappearance of the cock. On the next page we are told of Mr Snagsby getting such a 'flavour' of the country out of telling his apprentices of times when a clear brook once ran down Holborn, and Turnstile really was a turnstile, 'that he never wants to go there'. Again, the sentence slowly evolves towards its perversely surprising conclusion. Passages of mellow humour, often identifying with the characters (e.g. the Bagnets and Mr Snagsby), rather than getting at them (Mrs Snagsby), are surprisingly frequent in the omniscient narrative: they form a bridge to the enjoyment Esther clearly gets out of people and life.

More characteristic of the omniscient narrator, are flights of sustained **satire** and invective whenever he lays into Chancery, fashion, politicians, aristocrats, moneylenders, etc., but these passages, too, are richly entertaining. Perhaps it takes a warped sense of humour to find the omniscient narrator's treatment of the Smallweed family, or of Vholes's office, as hilarious as they are grotesque.

The omniscient narrative employs satire, **irony** and humour, and sometimes all at once. Esther, generally speaking, develops from one who responds with humour (with its inescapable connotations of 'good humour') to people and incidents (Peepy with his head stuck in the railings), to one who occasionally indulges in irony. On Chancery for instance, she pulls herself up for using the term 'progress': 'the case in progress – if I may use a phrase so ridiculous in such a connexion' (p. 397).

In some scenes Esther is both a character and a satirical device, 'the innocent eye', through whom the author pursues his own satirical purpose. Describing Mrs Pardiggle, diffidently, she introduces a formidable lady who seems to need a lot of room. 'And she really did, for she knocked down little chairs with her skirts that were quite a great way off' (p. 124). Much of what Mrs Pardiggle says involves self-satire, and Esther merely reports it 'innocently'. But Esther's response to Mrs Pardiggle's demand for her assistance in her 'visiting rounds' is a superb instance of satire through an innocent eye. Esther brings out Mrs Pardiggle's unfitness for charitable work by modestly listing her own lack of qualifications. She protests:

> That I was inexperienced in the art of adapting my mind to minds very differently situated ... That I had not that delicate knowledge of the heart which must be essential to such a work. That I had much to learn, myself, before I could teach others ... For these reasons, I thought it best to be as useful as I could, and to render what kind services I could, to those immediately about me; and to try to let that circle of duty gradually and naturally expand itself. All this I said, with anything but confidence; because Mrs Pardiggle was much older than I, and had great experience, and was so very military in her manners. (Chapter 8, p. 128)

Underlying this irony is a moral positive associated with Thomas Carlyle. In *Sartor Resartus*, he wrote: '*Do the duty which lies nearest thee*, which thou knowest to be a duty, thy second duty will already have become clearer.' That is, unconsciously, Esther is the vehicle for a moral critique of Mrs Pardiggle (and Mrs Jellyby) for failing to heed this message of Dickens's favourite Victorian prophet (see Background). But the satire is wholly in character, and, surely, wholly innocent of satiric intent. Even the picture of the stolidly miserable infant Pardiggle 'voluntarily enrolled ... in the Infant Bonds of Joy' is in Mrs Pardiggle's own words.

There are, of course subtler dimensions of irony, not detectable in the language of a particular passage, but in the larger course of events or of characters. In a long novel about a court case, Jarndyce and Jarndyce, we no doubt expect to find out what it was all about, even if Richard doesn't live long enough: but as D. A. Miller has pointed out (see Further Reading, on Deconstruction) we, like Richard, are victims of vain expectations. We never find out what the true will was, because the case just stops when costs have consumed the entire bequest. It is characteristic of Dickens to play such games with his readers, and he often does so with characters.

A favourite game is to manoeuvre the reader into passing judgement on characters who turn out not to be guilty of what we suspect them of. He plays the game rather obviously with Lady Dedlock (vis-à-vis the murder of Tulkinghorn) and more subtly with Sir Leicester. We are allowed to spend more than half the novel laughing at Sir Leicester – a regular butt of the·narrator's satire, especially for his aristocratic narrowness and old-fashioned attitudes – before the same character becomes the vehicle for a deeper critique of Victorian society's moral narrowness. When he voices his 'full forgiveness' and speaks of being 'on unaltered terms' with Lady Dedlock, he is likely to leave the implied (Victorian) reader feeling uncomfortable: who is this old dinosaur to challenge the cruel sexual mores of Victorian England?

CHARACTERS & CHARACTERISATION

Dickens has a knack of giving characters precisely as much life or 'roundness' as they need for their function in his novel. A 'round' character, as defined by E. M. Forster, in his classic *Aspects of the Novel*, is likely to be complex and capable of development, or decline. We know their inner lives. Oddly enough there are rather few of these in *Bleak House*, apart from Esther herself, and although we are told a lot about her there is much that remains mysterious. Other characters can be complex but static: Skimpole, for instance, doesn't change but it may take us a while to read him correctly and we experience some of Esther's confusion here. 'Flat' characters can be reliably wholesome (Mrs Bagnet in her grey cloak), or repellently evil (Grandfather Smallweed). Others seem to be just as 'flat' to begin with, but come to life when needed, like Sir Leicester Dedlock in the instance just cited.

LADY DEDLOCK, we know from the beginning, is more vulnerable and more transparent than she likes people to think. She possesses a force of character that is admired by both Tulkinghorn and Esther, and she is worshipped by Lawrence Boythorn. But the vivid phrase by which her response to social success is captured – 'she fell, not into the melting but rather into the freezing mood' (p. 22) – prepares us at once, as does the lengthy depiction of her childlessness and her boredom, to expect some climactic outbursts of passion, fatally impulsive acts, and revelations concerning a life of repression. SIR LEICESTER promises no such revelations, yet he progresses from a cipher to a man. Oddly, in fact, by the end of the novel he seems to stand for exactly what Lady Dedlock has betrayed in herself (except in her tell-tale adoption of Rosa, her maid), namely a life lived according to love. The character introduced in Chapter 2 gives no sign of such development. Later on, incidentally, he seems less honourable than the caricature (in 'National and Domestic' we are made aware of his complicity in a network of political corruption and we may wonder if Dickens remembered having credited him with truthfulness and integrity on p. 22). In 'The Ironmaster' he is shown as a dinosaur in an age of social mobility. Yet in Chapters 54 and 58 moving testimonials to his side of the marriage remind us that 'he married her for love' (p. 22). The reader is not allowed to rest in one estimate of Sir Leicester.

Bleak House creates Dickens's new mode of the brilliantly ambiguous character, especially in his most topical creation, MR BUCKET. The plain-clothes detective branch was first created in 1844 and one might expect a purely realistic treatment. In fact, from his first introduction into the novel he seems to belong to the world of fable more than that of naturalism. He materialises before an astonished Snagsby; he seems able to project himself in different forms (he makes his victims see him as a doctor in the scene at Gridley's death); waiting for Esther towards the end he mounts a tall tower in his mind and scans the countryside for Lady Dedlock. He is courteous, affable, and apparently well-meaning; yet worldly wise to the verge of cynicism. What motivates him, whom he really serves, and what ultimate values he represents, may be very hard to pin down. He is described in Chapter 53 as 'mildly studious in his observation of human nature, on the whole a benignant philosopher, inclined not to be severe on the follies of mankind'; yet as Volumnia perceives, he is 'charmingly *horrible*'. As A. E. Dyson observes, he is usually fatal to those he pursues.

JARNDYCE himself shares some of this disturbingly ambiguous quality. Sometimes he is simply the epitome of decency; sometimes he is Dickens's voice (as in the marvellous denunciation of Chancery in Chapter 8); sometimes he seems morally blind. He spends a life making amends for being caught up in a system of property which links him – ultimately – to a row of houses in Tom-all-Alone's. Is he 'The Good Man in Victorian Society' as Q. D. Leavis suggests? We are assured by Ada (p. 59) that in her mother's eyes, 'the noble generosity of his character ... was to be trusted above all earthly things', and certainly his halo gets brighter and brighter until he is almost transfigured into sainthood at the close. Yet this critic of organised philanthropy sometimes treats both Charley and Esther as parcels; and it is odd, some critics have argued, that he has the effrontery to lecture Richard on the importance of vocation, while having none himself, and sheltering the monstrous parasite, Skimpole, who has no sense of vocation at all.

In *Bleak House* numerous characters seem to be versions of each other, constituting an infinite series of variations on particular themes. With a little ingenuity you could probably arrange them all, like beads on a necklace (to use Esther's image), or linked hand in hand in a dance of death, or a giant mamba. Mrs Jellyby, as a philanthropist, is comparable to the altogether more organised and less affable Mrs Pardiggle whose habit of talking of people and delivering meaningless moralities is later echoed in Mr Chadband's self-regarding flights of **rhetoric** on Jo. The two women exist to satirise 'telescopic philanthropy' and 'rapacious benevolence', especially when allied with neglect or exploitation of children. Unlike the two women, however, who have good intentions, Chadband is a monstrous piece of humbug: he even joins the blackmailing party at the close of the Dedlock story. Harold Skimpole treats Jo with even less humanity than Chadband, and Skimpole's wife is treated just as Mr Turveydrop's was. Both forms of exploitation are subtler forms of oppression than the treatment of Jenny and her friend by the brutal brickmakers, whose violence is echoed in Punch and Judy fashion by Grandfather Smallweed's constant attacks on Grandmother

Y

Smallweed. These unaccountable fits of belligerence are **analogous** to those of Gridley, the man from Shropshire (whose agony is shared by Miss Flite, whose own 'madness' portends that of Richard) and to those of Boythorn, whose comic feud with Sir Leicester mirrors Hortense's passion for revenge (both Boythorn's and Hortense's rage may be equally rooted in sexual energies). And so on.

Jo is in some ways the central character of *Bleak House*, simply because he embodies injustice and carries disease, and because he connects almost all the main characters, and reveals them in their true lights. For instance, Nemo (the law-writer) and Snagsby (the law-stationer) both appear as Jarndyce figures – stepfathering and befriending Jo, just as Jarndyce fosters Esther. Snagsby and Jarndyce endlessly hand out more money, to no more ultimate effect. Jo, as victim, exposes both Chadband and Skimpole, who sells him to Inspector Bucket. He exposes the ambiguity or moral nullity of various agents of the law: the policeman (endlessly urging him to move on); the detective (who pursues him for no good reason except that Tulkinghorn wants him to) and Tulkinghorn himself who merely uses him to incriminate Lady Dedlock. He reveals, on the other hand, the practical goodness of an amazing range of genuinely benevolent characters, including the eccentric Miss Flite, the surgeon Mr Woodcourt, and Trooper George, as well as Esther, Guster and Phil Squod (orphans like himself). As an illiterate child, munching his breakfast on the doorstep of the Society for the Propagation of the Gospel in Foreign Parts, Jo illustrates most fully the wickedness, as Dickens sees it, of 'telescopic philanthropy'. Innocently, he observes the likeness of Esther to Lady Dedlock, whom he has led to the pauper's grave of her dead lover. As an innocent plague carrier, he carries the smallpox that visits upon Esther the 'sins' of her mother. He is tended in his final hours, dying of smallpox, by the surprisingly motherly Trooper George, who has spent much of his life as a sort of voluntary orphan, but who ends the novel as resident male nurse to that embodiment of aristocracy, the stricken Sir Leicester Dedlock. All of which is to say, that in reading *Bleak House*, the name of the game is not so much sketching individual characters as following the analogies and the relationships.

At the heart of modern readings of the novel, undoubtedly, is ESTHER. Once thought static and insipid, or an inconsistent mask (through whom we see Dickens himself when she has anything funny or penetrating to say, as if she were really 'not very clever'), Esther has been recognised in recent readings as one who is capable of very individual and very shrewd insights. Early in the novel, as in the treatment of Mrs Pardiggle or Krook, she deferentially attributes some of her sharpest observations to others. But it is she (rather than Jarndyce), who condemns Skimpole's worldliness. By Chapter 37 she is capable of advising Richard; and in Chapter 38 she cuts sharply through Guppy's equivocations. In advising Richard she assumes the functions of guardianship. In fact, she takes the initiative surprisingly often in conversations where Jarndyce is silently present (almost as silent as Mr Jellyby). 'Angel in the house', in any exact sense of that term, she decidedly is not. She represents a decisiveness and moral force that compensates for the lack of it in Richard or even in Jarndyce. Yet at the same time she is marked by reticence, self-deprecation, and an irritating habit of constantly apologising for talking about herself. In some ways, one may feel, Dickens has it both ways with Esther: we are clearly meant to *admire* her capacity for self-sacrifice, while feeling that it is both pathological (induced by her godmother's cruel morality) and *wrong*. It is right that she is rewarded with happiness and sexual fulfilment: yet in a curious way she seems to have deserved both by renouncing either of them as hers by right.

RICHARD's fate is foreshadowed from the outset by Miss Flite and by Gridley. His lack of judgement, compared with Esther, comes out in his being 'fascinated', i.e. lulled, by Skimpole, even while being exploited by him: 'what a fascinating child it is' (p. 593). Like Skimpole he exhibits a fatal lack of any clear sense of vocation, though he is distinguished from Skimpole by having a conscience, and by being generous rather than calculating. Dickens develops the fatally languid character, incapable of decisive commitment, in James Harthouse (*Hard Times*) and Eugene Wrayburn (*Our Mutual Friend*).

The most malign presence in the novel (apart from the comic Smallweed) is TULKINGHORN. Lady Dedlock gives us one insight into his motivation: his calling, she says, is 'the acquisition of secrets, and the holding possession of such power as they give him' (p. 581). But the omniscient narrator tells us in Chapter 16 that he is fiercely misogynist: 'There are women enough in the world, Mr

Tulkinghorn thinks – too many; they are at the bottom of all that goes wrong in it' (and Tulkinghorn confirms this comment in Chapter 41, p. 658).

GUPPY, though amiable and comic, and only a small fish ('Guppy' means gossipy, usually, but is also the name of a small fish that thrives in polluted waters), clearly has on a smaller scale the tenacity and the forensic instincts of Tulkinghorn. He is socially inept, and the absurd commercial and legal jargon in his proposal scene with Esther is a scene of high comedy. Clearly his refusal of money from Lady Dedlock is sincere, but the mere fact that he is upwardly mobile in the legal profession is enough to make one suspect Guppy of being less amiable and disinterested than he appears. His conduct towards Esther is a strange mixture of 'the tender passion' and the calculation of a man on the make.

KROOK is perhaps more a device than a character: he concentrates the smouldering antagonism of the law to all that lives and moves, collecting hair, skins, rags, and bones. From the moment of his introduction he seems destined for spontaneous combustion, seeming 'on fire within'. His function is to embody the acquisitive, collecting, devouring instincts, which, in the real Lord Chancellor, are obscured by dignity and affability. He clearly wants to add Ada's hair to his collection the moment he sees it; and his decision not to skin his own cat is motivated more by regard for the usefulness of her claws than by any kindliness. He enjoys the feeling that he holds the key to Jarndyce and Jarndyce, but will not part with the secret while it may profit anyone else. Is he a harmless eccentric? Or does his chuckling 'All's fish that comes to my net' indicate relish for the business of harvesting the hopes (and the remains) of men and women? He is such an indispensable part of the **symbolism** of the book that when he spontaneously combusts another figure has to take his place: namely Vholes.

All the lawyers, and their strange counterpart, Krook, are marked by a slow fixed way of looking at their clients, a sinister quality that is made most cannibalistic or vampirish in the lifeless VHOLES. 'A *most* respectable man', Vholes pursues his profession, which is to extract whatever can be extracted from his clients, in order to support 'a father in the Vale of Taunton, and three daughters at home' (p. 622). He shores up the system, and the system loyally shores up Mr Vholes. Any proposal to reform the wasteful practices of law, the narrator tells us, meets with the objection, what is to become of Vholes? 'As though, Mr Vholes and his relations being minor cannibal chiefs, and it being proposed to abolish cannibalism, indignant champions were to put the case thus: Make man-eating unlawful, and you starve the Vholeses!' (pp. 622–3). Meanwhile blue bags in his office, stuffed out of shape, lie like 'the larger sort of serpents in their first gorged state', and Mr Vholes steadily watches his client while 'the official cat is patiently watching a mouse's hole'. Explicitly in Chapter 60 Esther observes 'something of the Vampire in him'.

MR TURVEYDROP, the professor of deportment, works his son (as he worked his wife) to exhaustion, while condescending to deport himself quite beautifully, in homage to the Prince Regent. Esther says, when she first meets his son, Prince Turveydrop, that 'I received the impression that he was like his mother, and that his mother had not been much considered or well used'. Esther responds negatively to his 'disagreeable gallantry' (p. 229) and notes with pleasure (p. 773) that 'he had ceased to be particular in his attentions since I had been so altered'.

He is analogous to HAROLD SKIMPOLE, the cynical aesthete, who exploits Esther and Richard shamelessly on their first meeting, and is cruelly indifferent to the sufferings of the Neckett children and of Jo, other than as subjects for poetry. Skimpole is a man of style who lives for himself and on his friends. He mystifies Esther from the start: how could he be so free of the accountabilities of life? He talks brilliantly, reasons himself out of any sense of duty quite amazingly, and can sometimes produce a brilliant summing up of other characters, such as the warm-hearted blunderbuss Lawrence Boythorn ('Nature forgot to shade him off, I think? ... A little too boisterous, like the sea?' p. 241). But this man who can sing affecting ballads about orphan children, yet betray the feverish orphan Jo for 'a fypunnote', has also reduced his long-suffering wife to an invalid, and given his daughters just enough education 'to be their father's playthings in his idlest hours' (pp. 676, 679). As the novel progresses, the early impression of childish irresponsibility darkens to a sense of evil and the reader is likely first to weary of Skimpole, and then to judge him ever more harshly. It is hard to think of Dickens as a reader of theology, but in 1843, in a work called *Either-Or*, the Danish theologian Søren Kierkegaard epitomised existential choice as lying between an Aesthetic and an Ethical approach to existence, precisely the choice posed by the pairing of Skimpole and Esther.

GRANDFATHER SMALLWEED, though animated enough to throw cushions at his wife, is little more than a cushion himself and has to be constantly shaken up by his daughter Judy, and carried about by others, one of numerous lame patriarchs in the novel. This doesn't prevent him exploding verbally, like a grotesque lower-middle-class version of the gouty Sir Leicester. Whether addressing his wife ('you brimstone chatterer', p. 338) or Trooper George ('I'll smash you. I'll crumble you. I'll powder you.' p. 547) this stunted little man's life energy is perverted to avarice, malice and calculation.

MISS FLITE, small, birdlike, and keeper of birds, is characterised by a speech pattern, as are most of the other characters. Her speech hops in short phrases from point to point: 'I had youth and hope. I believe, beauty. It matters very little now … I have the honour to attend court regularly. With my documents. I expect a judgment. Shortly' (p. 47). Miss Flite's eccentricity is altogether more affecting than the grotesque Krook or Smallweed, and as a victim of Chancery her 'mad' language carries much of Dickens's symbolism. In Chapter 1 the comment that she carries some litter in a reticule 'which she calls her documents' implies that she shares Dickens's method of **ironising** through **metaphor**. Her birds, named in Chapter 14 and released in Chapter 65, are nonetheless captives, and she seems at times an abused abuser. As she says of Richard in Chapter 60: 'next to myself he is the most constant suitor in court. He begins quite to amuse our little party. Ve-ry friendly little party are we not?'

MRS BAGNET, of all the married women in the novel, is the one who meets with the third-person narrator's most evident approval. A strong resourceful woman, she is capable of finding her way home from foreign parts, 'with nothing but a grey cloak and an umbrella'; manages her household uncomplainingly, has brought up three children, makes up her husband's mind for him, on every day of the year except her birthday, and has developed a capital sum of sixpence into a successful music shop. The affable Mr Bagnet, or Lignum vitae (wood, or staff of life), is no more than an appendage to Mrs Bagnet: he knows his inferiority, but as the nominal commanding officer of his little unit will not admit to it, as 'discipline must be maintained'.

CHARACTERS & CHARACTERISATION continued

CADDY JELLYBY, when we first meet her, is in a dreadful state of ink, frayed slippers, and disgruntlement, with nothing about her in its proper place or condition. She has been so neglected by her mother that she needs a thorough course in domestic management before she marries Prince Turveydrop. Yet she copes with a deaf-mute child, progresses from dancing-master's wife to mistress of a dancing academy, taking over from her weak husband and his lame father, and eventually rides about in her own carriage. Pointedly, given the novel's concern with gender issues, Esther always calls Caddy by her maiden name.

THE ROUNCEWELLS include three of the most solid characters in the book, the attractive loyal Trooper (always sitting so as to accommodate an imaginary sword, stroking an imaginary moustache, or jingling imaginary spurs), his mother, the professional housekeeper, soul of loyalty and service to the Dedlocks but ultimately most loyal to her sons (she will bring down the Dedlocks if need be to clear George's name), and the Ironmaster, whose quiet self-assurance and dignity makes him the new man counterposed to Sir Leicester's embodiment of aristocracy in its dotage.

IMAGERY & SYMBOLISM

This note has pointed repeatedly to the astonishing range of associated **images** deployed throughout the novel, from the opening fog and mud, through documents, ink, parchment, detritus, disease, pox, waste, death, decay, corruption, entropy, grease, skin, cannibalism, fire. Clusters of such images are blent together in **symbolic** patterns suggestive of entropy or apocalypse.

Interestingly, the two narrators share responsibility for working in this way. In describing Krook's shop (pp. 67–8), Esther's mode may seem more passive than the other narrator's: simply listing, it seems, what she sees. His description of Nemo's room at the end of Chapter 10 is more linguistically vivid. It opens with 'soot, and grease and dirt', and proceeds to develop the theme of death through such **metaphors** as 'the rusty skeleton of a grate', a portmanteau collapsing 'like the cheeks of a starved man', a 'perishing' mat, and a candle that has guttered down into 'a tower of winding sheet'. But Esther is capable of *initiating* aspects of the novel's symbolic method, and confirming others. The third-person narrator calls at the end of Chapter 1 for Chancery and all its injustice to be burnt away 'in a great funeral pyre': Esther – awaiting audience with the Lord Chancellor in Chapter 3 – sits beside 'candles burning with a white flame, and looking raw and cold', and the Chancery fire 'burning, burning, burning', and sees Ada and Richard for the first time 'standing near a great, loud-roaring fire'. Richard sees it as a drowsy Chancery lion, but Esther has already introduced the theme of combustion without heat.

In Chapter 5 it is again Richard who fancies that the bones in Krook's shop are the bones of clients, thus alerting the reader to Krook's as a processing plant (where Ada's hair, like Lady Jane's skin, are perceived as potential additions to the accumulation of sacks of hair, heaped skin, piled bones that constitute the horror of the place) but it is Esther who describes Krook as 'on fire within', yet cold without. She reports his self-perception as a marine version of the grim reaper: 'I've a liking for rust and must and cobwebs. And all's fish that comes to my net'. In Chapter 39 the third-person narrator matches this stroke with Vholes 'making hay of the grass which is flesh'. By then, Esther, in Chapter 37, has already seen him as 'a sallow man with pinched lips that looked as if they were cold, a red eruption here and there upon his face, tall and thin', and noted how this man of impaired digestion conveys Richard to Jarndyce and Jarndyce behind 'a gaunt pale horse'. The third-person narrator borrows Esther's description of his lifeless manner and inward way of speaking, and confirms Esther's insight that Vholes is the reincarnation of Krook and another manifestation of the grim reaper. The third-person narrator's cannibal imagery in 'Attorney and Client' (Chapter 39) only makes explicit Esther's already established alarm at Vholes's way of looking at Richard in Chapter 37. And Esther is given the last word: when Vholes departs, at the end of the suit, 'he gave one gasp as if he had swallowed the last morsel of his client, and his black buttoned-up unwholesome figure glided away to the low door at the end of the hall' (p. 976). Mr Vholes is returning to the underworld perhaps?

Caddy's frayed slippers (Chapter 4) and Nemo's perishing mat, decomposing into rope yarn (Chapter 10), link up with the vision Esther has at Deal, of 'a few early ropemakers, who, with the yarn twisted around their bodies, looked as if … they were spinning themselves into cordage'

(p. 699). The three images express the theme of entropy: slippers, mats and people, all turning or returning into rope; things returning to their elements; people turning into thinginess; life and structure breaking down. In this rich text, so full of characters and themes and incidents and mysteries that it seems ready to fall apart at the seams, you will find that Dickens's poetic imagination provides the most surprising and insistent trains of imagery to hold it together.

LANGUAGE & STYLE

NARRATIVE STYLE

> He has some manuscript near him, but is not referring to it. With the round top of an inkstand and two broken bits of sealing-wax, he is silently and slowly working out whatever train of indecision is in his mind …
>
> The red bit [of sealing wax], the black bit, the inkstand top, the other inkstand top, the little sand-box. So! You to the middle, you to the right, you to the left. This train of indecision must surely be worked out now or never. – Now! Mr Tulkinghorn gets up, adjusts his spectacles, puts on his hat, puts the manuscript in his pocket, goes out … (p. 159)

Dickens is often accused of being brilliant at describing the surfaces of things, and what people do, or say, or look like, but having little gift for depths of feeling. His love scenes are inadequate or embarrassing but his buildings inimitably expressive. This passage is an example of how Dickens turns this weakness into strength. It describes Mr Tulkinghorn's realisation that in order to unravel the mystery of Lady Dedlock's interest in the piece of writing she saw in Chapter 2, he must visit Snagsby's law stationer shop to ascertain the name and address of the law-writer. It is much to the point that we should be left guessing what Mr Tulkinghorn is up to, so that we have to second-guess the author and work it out ourselves. It is also part of the characterisation that Tulkinghorn appears to have no interest in the manuscript (the tell-tale piece of writing) and that no glimpse of his motivation or his reasoning is allowed to pass the mute exterior. Yet the passage conveys the relentless concentrated purpose of the man; and dramatises the fact that his apparent immobility does not make him incapable of sudden and decisive action. Arriving at

Snagsby's on the next page ('as the crow flies') he finds the answer he is looking for before Snagsby can find his way through his own ledger.

NAME & SPEECH SIGNATURES

Tulkinghorn's name manages to suggest something rather antiquated, rather dangerous, inclined to stalk his prey, and aggressively masculine. Something of the same qualities adhere to Boythorn, though with a mixture of innocence. A name like Dedlock is obviously **symbolic**: Turveydrop, on the other hand, slyly pokes fun at the character by having about it more than a hint of excremental droppings as well as street songs ('Turvey, Turvey ...'). Esther is the name of a biblical queen who redeemed her people, while Summerson tells us something about the love between her parents, something very different from her Aunt Barbary, whose name recalls a very prickly evergreen. Jarndyce, oddly, is given a name which (since it is close to the nineteenth-century pronunciation of jaundice) describes the effect of the Jarndyce and Jarndyce suit on everybody but himself. Weevle, who is despatched by Guppy to find what he can on the premises of Krook, is named after a small insect that spends its life eating its way through flour and grains – the raw materials of mills (the ever-working mills of the law). Most of the names in the novel work in one or other of these ways; directly symbolic, or subtly apt.

There is not space to list and analyse the speech signatures Dickens gives to many of his characters. Among the most inventive is that of Jo:

> 'They're wot's left, Mr Sangsby', says Jo, 'out of a sov'ring as wos give me by a lady in a wale as sed she wos a servant ... and asked to be showd this 'ere ouse and the ouse wot him as you give the writin to died at, and the berrin ground wot he's berrid in.' (Chapter 19)

Compare this with Lady Dedlock on page 261:

> 'Can you shew me all those places ...? The place he wrote for, the place he died at, the place where you were taken to, and the place where he was buried?'

Lady Dedlock's speech is simple but entirely grammatical and elegantly balanced. Jo's flattened vowel in 'wot' shows that he has no conception of a system of writing in which such sounds are rendered 'what'. His dyslexic version of Snagsby, his grammatical helter-skelter through 'the house wot him as you give the writin to died at', and his contraction of burying and buried are perfect. Norman Page cites this passage as part of a discussion, well worth reading, in *Speech in the English Novel* (1988) where he gives examples of Dickens's endless care to get the sound of his characters exactly right, especially when dealing with dialect.

Comic characters, such as Guppy and Snagsby, are usually given speech characteristics – combining inappropriate registers in Guppy's case, or habits of hesitancy in Snagsby's – that mark them immediately. This novel, as part of its treatment of Dandyism, specialises in characters with elevated but unintentionally funny versions of heightened **rhetoric**. Conversation Kenge, for instance, models his delivery on that of a great lord. He assures Mr Jarndyce that 'We are a great country ... a very great country' and 'Would you wish a great system to have a little system? Now really, really!' As he speaks he moves his right hand 'as if it were a silver trowel to spread the cement of his words on the structure of the system, and consolidate it for a thousand ages' (p. 950). Chadband, similarly, climbs what the narrator calls 'staircases of rhetoric': 'May this house live upon the fatness of the land; may corn and wine be plentiful therein; may it grow, may it thrive, may it prosper, may it advance, may it proceed, may it press forward!' (p. 313) (which this sentence clearly does not). Sir Leicester's sentences also circle grandly and pompously without making much progress, but his speech rarely falls into the utterly vacuous style of Kenge or the vulgar unctuousness of Chadband, whose ludicrousness comes out in his comic pronunciations: 'terewth', 'untoe', 'air we'. They are **analogous** to, but could not be mistaken for, each other.

Timing is of the essence, as in Sir Leicester's wonderful response to the Ironmaster (p. 454) where, as so often, the narrative interpolations provide the dramatic pauses in delivery:

> Sir Leicester's magnificence explodes. Calmly, but terribly.
>
> 'Mr Rouncewell,' says Sir Leicester, with his right hand in the breast of his blue coat – the attitude of state in which he is painted in the gallery: 'do you draw a parallel between Chesney Wold, and a –' here he resists a disposition to choke – 'a factory?'

ALLUSION & POETIC PROSE

Whether in tribute to the literary knowledge of his readers, or to amuse himself at a different level while amusing them, Dickens indulged in an extraordinary amount of literary and biblical **allusion**. Esther is constantly quoting her Bible (and her Victorian readers would have picked up all the references). But the third-person narrator draws widely on poetry, especially Shakespeare, Wordsworth and Coleridge, and frequently drips into poetic rhythms himself. To give just a few examples, all in **iambic pentameter**:

- Chancery we are told, in Chapter 1, '*so overthrows the brain and breaks the heart*' that one would suffer any wrong rather than come there. Wordsworth, in his poem 'Michael' writes that love can make a thing endurable that else '*would overset the brain and break the heart*'.
- Lady Dedlock is presented in Chapter 2, '*with all her perfections on her head*'. This is Shakespeare, but with a tell-tale missing beat: Hamlet wishes to slay Claudius not while he is praying but '*with all his imperfections on his head*'. The allusion alerts us to Lady Dedlock's hidden 'sin'.
- Describing the death of Jo the narrator drops (unconsciously, Dickens claimed) into an iambic pentameter of his own to conclude his indictment of Queen Victoria, protesting that while government fiddles, the poor are dying '*and dy/ing thus/ around/ us ev/ery day*'.

In so grim a book, it is surprising to find so much beauty. There are wonderfully lyrical passages of sustained poetic prose, for instance in the introduction of Lady Dedlock (see Textual Analysis, Text 1) or the interlude before the death of Tulkinghorn. But apart from these big 'set pieces' he frequently ends his chapters with a beautifully turned, rhythmic reprise. At random one might pick this pair, one from each narrative, in successive chapters:

> Still, very steadfastly and quietly walking towards it [the House], a peaceful figure too in the landscape, went Mademoiselle Hortense, shoeless, through the wet grass (p. 300).
>
> There he sits, the sun going down, the river running fast, the crowd flowing by him in two streams – everything moving on to some purpose and to one end – until he is stirred up, and told to 'move on' too (p. 315).

Esther, here, is drawing the venom from the previous description (by the keeper's wife) of Hortense walking through the wet grass as if wading through blood. Since Hortense is sometimes thought to embody, as a 'double', the repressed passions of both Lady Dedlock and Esther, this muted, pacifying representation is much in Esther's character. In the second quotation the third-person narrator is compressing into an evening image the theme of his chapter, which concerns the plight of Jo, harried by Bucket and Tulkinghorn and Chadband, yet not belonging at all to their social worlds, and being compelled to 'move on' but with no 'end' to reach.

Rhetoric

It is partly through Carlyle's influence, I suspect, that Dickens exploits a greater range of styles than is usually permissible in a novel: along with passages of poetic (symbolic) description, and full-scene dramatic presentation, and the conventional summary style of narration, Dickens also employs devices alien to the realist novel. He is adept at journalistic **reportage** (a sort of shorthand representation of dialogue). He also enjoys the orator's or storyteller's involvement of narrator and reader in present tense reactions to sights and sounds, as for instance:

> O horror, he IS here! and this, from which we run away, striking out the light and overturning one another into the street [Guppy, Jobling, Dickens, you and I] is all that represents him.
>
> Help, help, help! come into this house for Heaven's sake. (p. 519)

From this extraordinary passage about the remains of Krook, Dickens moves straight into a heightened, rhythmic, **rhetorical** finale to the chapter, representing spontaneous combustion as the desired end to all Lord Chancellors and all Courts.

PART FOUR

TEXTUAL ANALYSIS

TEXT 1 (from CHAPTER 2, 'IN FASHION')

My Lady Dedlock has returned to her house in town for a few days previous to her departure for Paris, where her ladyship intends to stay some weeks; after which her movements are uncertain. The fashionable intelligence says so, for the comfort of the Parisians, and it knows all fashionable things. To know things otherwise, were to be unfashionable. My Lady Dedlock has been down at what she calls, in familiar conversation, her 'place' in Lincolnshire. The waters are out in Lincolnshire. An arch of the bridge in the park has been sapped and sopped away. The adjacent low-lying ground, for half a mile in breadth, is a stagnant river, with melancholy trees for islands in it, and a surface punctured all over, all day long, with falling rain. My Lady Dedlock's 'place' has been extremely dreary. The weather, for many a day and night, has been so wet that the trees seem wet through, and the soft loppings and prunings of the woodman's axe can make no crash or crackle as they fall. The deer, looking soaked, leave quagmires, where they pass. The shot of a rifle loses its sharpness in the moist air, and its smoke moves in a tardy little cloud towards the green rise, coppice-topped, that makes a background for the falling rain. The view from my Lady Dedlock's own windows is alternately a lead-coloured view, and a view in Indian ink. The vases on the stone terrace in the foreground catch the rain all day; and the heavy drops fall, drip, drip, drip, upon the broad flagged pavement, called, from old time, the Ghost's Walk, all night. On Sundays, the little church in the park is mouldy; the oaken pulpit breaks out into a cold sweat; and there is a general smell and taste as of the ancient Dedlocks in their graves. My Lady Dedlock (who is childless), looking out in the early twilight from her boudoir at a keeper's lodge, and seeing the light of a fire upon the latticed panes, and smoke rising from the chimney, and a child, chased by a woman, running out into the rain to meet the shining figure of a wrapped-up man coming through the gate, has been put quite out of temper. My Lady Dedlock says she has been 'bored to death.'

Therefore my Lady Dedlock has come away from the place in Lincolnshire, and has left it to the rain, and the crows, and the rabbits, and the deer, and the partridges and pheasants. The pictures of the Dedlocks past and gone have seemed to vanish into the damp walls in mere lowness of spirits, as the housekeeper has passed along the old rooms, shutting up the shutters. And when they will next come forth again, the fashionable intelligence – which, like the fiend, is omniscient of the past and present, but not the future – cannot yet undertake to say.

Sir Leicester Dedlock is only a baronet, but there is no mightier baronet than he. His family is as old as the hills, and infinitely more respectable. He has a general opinion that the world might get on without hills, but would be done up without Dedlocks. He would on the whole admit Nature to be a good idea (a little low, perhaps, when not enclosed with a park-fence), but an idea dependent for its execution on your great county families. He is a gentleman of strict conscience, disdainful of all littleness and meanness, and ready, on the shortest notice, to die any death you may please to mention rather than give occasion for the least impeachment of his integrity. He is an honourable, obstinate, truthful, high-spirited, intensely prejudiced, perfectly unreasonable man.

Compared with the vivid opening of Chapter 1, with its staccato sentence fragments, conspicuous present participles, insistent **symbolism** and overt **satire**, this passage strikes a quieter note, but it is no less virtuoso. The chapter opening assures us that the world of fashion 'is not so unlike the Court of Chancery, but that we may pass from the one scene to the other, as the crow flies', both being realms of archaic precedent and usage. The first sentence quoted seems, simultaneously, to be a **pastiche** of the deferential tones of a courtier and the style of a social diarist. By implication the narrator reduces the height of 'intelligence' to the purveyance of gossip, and uniform gossip at that ('to know things otherwise were to be unfashionable'). It also implies, quietly, that one likeness between the world of fashion and the world of Chancery, is that its principle activity consists in espionage – the gathering of 'intelligence'. The pastiche then gives way to a poetic evocation of the watery state of Chesney Wold, as a symbol of enervation and decay. Finally, we revert to a social tone. The narrator employs the languid style of social discourse when referring to the lowness of spirits of the Dedlock pictures, and the fashionable intelligence that 'cannot yet undertake to say', and then shifts into more animated conversational rhythms for his satirical portrait of Sir Leicester. This works partly by mockery ('but *infinitely* more respectable') and partly by mimicry of Sir Leicester's own unspeakable grandeur ('a little low perhaps', 'your great country families').

In the description of My Lady Dedlock's 'place' the emphasis is still upon inactivity and changelessness, except for the imperceptible processes of decay. In place of the fog, soot and mud of Chapter 1 we have water and mist, lead and Indian ink, and an accumulation of silent 'loppings and prunings' which beautifully echo the **onomatopoeic** sapping and sopping of the bridge. In place of pedestrians and carriages, we have a woodman, a keeper and deer, but again, they are **analogously** mired and muffled alike, almost becoming one element. Trees are like islands, and as wet through as the deer, which leave 'quagmires'; the park and river are merged, the bridge and trees are falling alike, and equally wet through. Esther will find Chesney Wold serene, but the omniscient narrator sees the silence of death and decay.

In Chapter 1 the second paragraph seemed filled with foreshadowing of characters and events to come. This paragraph, especially on a second reading of the novel seems even fuller of foreshadowings: the shot of a rifle foreshadows the death of Tulkinghorn (whom we have not yet met) and the customers at George's shooting gallery. The lead-coloured view and view in Indian ink looks back to the leaden-headed obstruction in Chapter 1 and the state of ink in which Esther will find Guppy and Caddy in Chapters 3 and 4. The 'drip, drip, drip' foreshadows the haunting step that will be heard increasingly as Lady Dedlock approaches exposure. Most clearly of all, the poignant picture of the 'bored' Lady Dedlock '(who is childless)' looking out at a nameless child, a cottage window, and a wrapped up man conveys all we need to know of this woman's repressed and sorrowful life and encourages us to look for her child and her lover as we read on.

Thematically, this passage establishes Chesney Wold as a symbol of decay in the ruling class, Lady Dedlock as a woman whose real life is hidden, and Sir Leicester as another leaden-headed old obstruction. Husband and wife are introduced by quite different techniques: we are given subtly symbolic implications concerning Lady Dedlock's buried life, and a flatly summarising caricature of Sir Leicester. Both however, as the prelude to this passage tells us, are 'wrapped up in too much jeweller's cotton and fine wool'. Their world is deaf and blind to 'the larger worlds' and is 'sometimes unhealthy for want of air'. Deeper themes come out in the curious way in which the fashionable intelligence is both anonymous and collective, and its life (and intelligence) less animated and less individual than the park's animal life, or even the portraits which pass into the walls to come forth at some indeterminate future date. Given Dickens's Romantic allegiances, the idea of Nature as 'a little low, perhaps, when not enclosed by a park-fence' is devastating.

It is a varied, really very beautiful piece of writing, with subtle shifts in tone. The poetic qualities of the landscape description, with its **alliterations, assonance** and repetitions, are obvious. Less obviously, we might compare two of the lists. The languid enumeration of the park's animal life, Lady Dedlock having left it 'to the rain, and the crows, and the rabbits, and the deer, and the partridges and pheasants' brings out Lady Dedlock's boredom. The exasperated summary of Sir Leicester as 'an honourable, obstinate, truthful, high-spirited, intensely prejudiced, perfectly unreasonable man' is tonally much sharper. Whereas one list drags itself along flatly, the other builds to a crescendo – the stressed first syllables in 'hónourable, óbstinate, trúthful', the parallel construction of qualifier and noun in 'high-spirited, intensely prejudiced', the tetchy alliteration on ts and ps, and the notably balanced rhythm in the final phrase 'PÉR fect-ly-un RÉA son-ab-le MÁN'. Chesney Wold may signify inertia – but it has no hold on the narrator.

TEXT 2   (from CHAPTER 32, 'THE APPOINTED TIME')

It is night in Lincoln's Inn – perplexed and troublous valley of the shadow of the law, where suitors generally find but little day – and fat candles are snuffed out in offices, and clerks have rattled down the crazy wooden stairs, and dispersed. The bell that rings at nine o'clock, has ceased its doleful clangour about nothing; the gates are shut; and the night-porter, a solemn warder with a mighty power of sleep, keeps guard in his lodge. From tiers of staircase windows, clogged lamps like the eyes of Equity, bleared Argus with a fathomless pocket for every eye and an eye upon it, dimly blink at the stars. In dirty upper casements, here and there, hazy little patches of candle-light reveal where some wise draughtsman and conveyancer yet toils for the entanglement of real estate in meshes of sheepskin, in the average ratio of about a dozen of sheep to an acre of land. Over which bee-like industry, these benefactors of their species linger yet, though office-hours be past: that they may give, for every day, some good account at last.

In the neighbouring court, where the Lord Chancellor of the Rag and Bottle shop dwells, there is a general tendency towards beer and supper. … [A lengthy passage concerning the evening gossip of Mrs Piper and Mrs Perkins, young Piper and young Perkins being abed, is here omitted]. Now, there is a sound of putting up shop-shutters in the court, and a smell as of the smoking of pipes; and shooting stars are seen in upper windows, further indicating retirement to rest. Now, too, the policeman begins to push at doors; to try fastenings; to be suspicious of bundles; and to administer his beat, on the hypothesis that everybody is either robbing or being robbed.

It is a close night, though the damp cold is searching too; and there is a laggard mist a little way up in the air. It is a fine steaming night to turn the slaughter-houses, the unwholesome trades, the sewerage, bad water, and burial grounds to account, and give the Registrar of Deaths some extra business. It may be something in the air – there is plenty in it – or it may be something in himself, that is in fault; but Mr Weevle, otherwise Jobling, is very ill at ease. He comes and goes, between his own room and the open street door, twenty times an hour. He has been doing so, ever since it fell dark. Since the Chancellor shut up his shop, which he did very early to-night, Mr Weevle has been down and up, and down and up (with a cheap tight velvet skull-cap on his head, making his whiskers look out of all proportion), oftener than before.

It is no phenomenon that Mr Snagsby should be ill at ease too; for he always is so, more or less, under the oppressive influence of the secret that is upon him. Impelled by the mystery, of which he is a partaker, and yet in which he is not a sharer, Mr Snagsby haunts what seems to be its fountain-head – the rag and bottle shop in the court. It has an irresistible attraction for him. Even now, coming round by the Sol's Arms with the intention of passing down the court, and out at the Chancery Lane end, and so terminating his unpremeditated after-supper stroll of ten minutes long from his own door and back again, Mr Snagsby approaches.

'What, Mr Weevle?' says the stationer, stopping to speak. 'Are *you* there?'

'Ay!' says Weevle. 'Here I am, Mr Snagsby.'

'Airing yourself, as I am doing, before you go to bed?' the stationer inquires.

'Why, there's not much air to be got here, and what there is, is not very freshening,' Weevle answers, glancing up and down the court.

'Very true, sir. Don't you observe,' says Mr Snagsby, pausing to sniff and taste the air a little; 'don't you observe, Mr Weevle, that you're – not to put too fine a point upon it – that you're rather greasy here, sir?'

> 'Why, I have noticed myself that there is a queer kind of flavour in the place to-
> night,' Mr Weevle rejoins. 'I suppose it's chops at the Sol's Arms.'
>
> 'Chops, do you think? Oh! – Chops, eh?' Mr Snagsby sniffs and tastes again.
> 'Well, sir, I suppose it is. But I should say their cook at the Sol wanted a little
> looking after. She has been burning 'em, sir! And I don't think;' Mr Snagsby sniffs
> and tastes again, and then spits and wipes his mouth; 'I don't think – not to put
> too fine a point upon it – that they were quite fresh, when they were shown the
> gridiron.'
>
> 'That's very likely. It's a tainting sort of weather.'
>
> 'It *is* a tainting sort of weather,' says Mr Snagsby; 'and I find it sinking to the
> spirits.'
>
> 'By George! *I* find it gives me the horrors,' returns Mr Weevle.

Again one notes the rhythms, though here they are Dickens at his most theatrical, stentorian and portentous. This is not surprising when one considers the function of this passage which is to set the scene for the dramatic discovery of the death of Krook. The sequence builds slowly from general scene-setting, to conveying the general atmosphere in the locality, including a wry passage of **anaphora**, contrasting the ideal notion of evening rest with the activities of policemen on the beat, to recalling the unease of Weevle, and the deeper unease of Mr Snagsby, until it brings these two characters together in what is (after so slow a build-up) a starting burst of dialogue. The whole is designed, in almost every particular, with the death of Krook, and the peculiar manner of that death, in mind.

This passage is characteristic of Dickens the performer. The opening syllables – 'It is night in Lincoln's Inn' – make a dramatic scene-setting gesture, as if saying 'Lo!', before the phrase 'perplexed and troublous valley of the shadow of the law' intones a **parody** of Psalm 23: 'Yea though I walk through the valley of the shadow of death, I will fear no evil for Thou art with me'. The derisory reference to the night bell, with 'its doleful clangour about nothing', introduces a Shakespearean reference to the night porter and his 'mighty power of sleep' (**alluding** to the drunken porter in Shakespeare's *Macbeth*, and therefore to sudden death). The phrasing of the whole paragraph, leading up to the pious image of lawyers as 'benefactors of their species' lingering over their labours 'that they may give, for every day, some good account at last' has an orotund quality that is designed to be savoured. This last long clause

is (in poetic metre) a **heptameter**, as is the first long phrase: 'perpléxed |
and tróub|lous vál|ley òf | the shá|dow óf | the láw' and in both, death is
much to the point.

The 'fat candles', sheepskin, bleared lamps, and the steaming night
belong to the primary register of **images** in the novel. Each time candles
are mentioned the association with mutton and grease becomes a little
more explicit, though the sequence is only completed in Chapter 39 ('the
nightly ... consumption of mutton fat in candles, and ... fretting of ...
skins in greasy drawers'). The brilliant image here of lawyers toiling for
'the entanglement of real estate in meshes of sheepskin, in the average
ratio of about a dozen of sheep to an acre of land' provides a recurring
theme. In Lincoln's Inn Fields we are told later, 'the sheep are all made
into parchment, the goats into wigs, and the pasture into chaff' (p. 661),
and in the lyrical passage leading up to the violent death of Tulkinghorn,
'the shepherds play on Chancery pipes that have no stop, and keep their
sheep in the fold by hook and by crook until they have shorn them
exceeding close' (p. 749). Psalm 23, incidentally, begins 'The Lord is my
Shepherd' so the passage starts by evoking the Good Shepherd, who
feeds his sheep, contrasting Him with legal shepherds who convert them
into parchment to entangle the land to feed themselves. Behind this
imagery lies Milton's angry attack in *Lycidas* (1637) on ecclesiastical
wolves disguised as shepherds feeding *on* their flocks.

This is not merely a 'close' and 'searching' night (a little like
Tulkinghorn?) but 'one to turn the slaughter-houses, the unwholesome
trades, the sewerage, bad water, and burial grounds to account, and give
the Registrar of Deaths some extra business'. This vivid catalogue of
insanitary conditions gives a glimpse of the author's campaigning anger,
and leads into the pun on 'account', whereby the pious pretensions of
Equity toiling 'to give some good account at last' are perverted into the
money-grubbing reality, in 'turning to account' whereby disease makes
'business' for the Registrar of deaths.

The two characters who are singly introduced (standing out from
the general tendency of Cook's Court 'to beer and supper') are both on
the periphery of the parallel investigations of Tulkinghorn and Guppy
into the connections between Lady Dedlock and Nemo. They are
accessories in something they do not understand. Weevle is deputising
for Guppy who has an appointment with Krook; Snagsby is drawn

against his will to Krook's as the centre of the mystery, the rag and bottle shop having an irresistible attraction to him, as Chancery itself does for Richard, and Miss Flite, and Gridley. Snagsby's mild manners and circumlocutious enquiries contrast with Weevle's more prosaic and direct responses. The contrast is brought out more by the narrator interrupting Mr Snagsby's own self-interruptions, so as to give the dialogue the perfect timing: 'Very true, sir. Don't you observe,' says Mr Snagsby, pausing to sniff and taste the air a little; 'don't you observe, Mr Weevle, that you're – not to put too fine a point upon it – that you're rather greasy here, sir?' Amusing though Snagsby's form of the question is, his own pausing to 'sniff and taste the air' will be especially disturbing if we remember from Chapter 2 the 'general smell and taste of the ancient Dedlocks in their graves'. On a second reading, Weevle's attribution of that smell and taste to chops at the Sol's Arms is a grim and macabre piece of **irony**: what these two evening conversationalists are quietly sniffing, tasting, and comparing notes on, like connoisseurs of fine wine, is not tainted chops but all that remains of Mr Krook apart from a patch of viscous slime. With this revelation in prospect, Snagsby's characteristically mild complaint, 'It *is* a tainting sort of weather ... and I find it sinking to the spirits' is rightly trumped by Weevle's 'By George! *I* find it gives me the horrors.'

TEXT 3 (from CHAPTER 38, 'A STRUGGLE' [ESTHER'S NARRATIVE])

'Miss Summerson,' said Mr Guppy, rising, 'this is indeed an Oasis. Mother, will you be so good as to put a chair for the other lady, and get out of the gang-way.'

Mrs Guppy, whose incessant smiling gave her quite a waggish appearance, did as her son requested; and then sat down in a corner, holding her pocket-handkerchief to her chest, like a fomentation, with both hands.

I presented Caddy, and Mr Guppy said that any friend of mine was more than welcome. I then proceeded to the object of my visit.

'I took the liberty of sending you a note, sir,' said I.

Mr Guppy acknowledged its receipt by taking it out of his breast pocket, putting it to his lips, and returning it to his pocket with a bow. Mr Guppy's mother was so diverted that she rolled her head as she smiled, and made a silent appeal to Caddy with her elbow.

'Could I speak to you alone for a moment?' said I.

Anything like the jocoseness of Mr Guppy's mother now, I think I never saw. She made no sound of laughter; but she rolled her head, and shook it, and put her handkerchief to her mouth, and appealed to Caddy with her elbow, and her hand, and her shoulder, and was so unspeakably entertained altogether that it was with some difficulty she could marshal Caddy through the little folding-door into her bed-room adjoining.

'Miss Summerson,' said Mr Guppy, 'you will excuse the waywardness of a parent ever mindful of a son's appiness. My mother, though highly exasperating to the feelings, is actuated by maternal dictates.'

I could hardly have believed that anybody could in a moment have turned so red, or changed so much, as Mr Guppy did when I now put up my veil.

'I asked the favour of seeing you for a few moments here,' said I, 'in preference to calling at Mr Kenge's, because, remembering what you said on an occasion when you spoke to me in confidence, I feared I might otherwise cause you some embarrassment, Mr Guppy.'

I caused him embarrassment enough as it was, I am sure. I never saw such faltering, such confusion, such amazement and apprehension.

'Miss Summerson,' stammered Mr Guppy, 'I – I – beg your pardon, but in our profession – we – we – find it necessary to be explicit. You have referred to an occasion, miss, when I – when I did myself the honour of making a declaration which –'

Something seemed to rise in his throat that he could not possibly swallow. He put his hand there, coughed, made faces, tried again to swallow it, coughed again, made faces again, looked all round the room, and fluttered his papers.

'A kind of a giddy sensation has come upon me, miss,' he explained, 'which rather knocks me over. I – er – a little subject to this sort of thing – er – By George!'

I gave him a little time to recover. He consumed it in putting his hand to his forehead and taking it away again, and in backing his chair into the corner behind him.

'My intention was to remark, miss,' said Mr Guppy, '– dear me – something bronchial, I think – hem! – to remark that you was so good on that occasion as to repel and repudiate that declaration. You – you wouldn't perhaps object to admit that? Though no witnesses are present, it might be a satisfaction to – to your mind if you was to put in that admission.'

'There can be no doubt,' said I, 'that I declined your proposal without any reservation or qualification whatever, Mr Guppy.'

[…]

'Thank you,' returned Mr Guppy. 'Very honourable, I am sure. I regret that my arrangements in life, combined with circumstances over which I have no control, will put it out of my power ever to fall back upon that offer, or to renew it in any shape or form whatever; but it will ever be a retrospect entwined – er – with friendship's bowers.'

This scene shows the hapless Guppy at his worst, and Esther at her most self-confident. She has gone to Mr Guppy's to request him to desist from his enquiries into her origins, which, to do him justice, he does. Guppy's language, as always, is a hopeless mixture of registers, inappositely combined. His 'Oasis' belongs to his general category of sentimental romantic diction, such as 'friendship's bowers', 'imprinted on my art', and 'the tender passion', but his address to his Mother 'to 'get out of the gang-way' and his assuring Esther that 'anyone's sense would shew 'em' that his former declaration was final and there terminated, are brusque and rude. He has an astonishing ability to manufacture catch-phrases on the spot. Thus 'circumstances beyond my control' – his **euphemism** for Esther's scarred face – becomes his standard phrase for this calamity in subsequent chapters. Aiming at elegance Guppy falls, inevitably, into the ridiculous: his pronunciation (art and appiness lack even an apostrophe where the 'h' should be) and his shaky grammar ('if you was') ought to warn him against attempting such **rhetorical** flights as suggesting that memories of his proposal 'will ever be a retrospect entwined – er – with friendship's bowers', but self-awareness is not his strong point. Perhaps Esther and Dickens are guilty of snobbery, but Guppy's real vulgarity and materialism come out in his incapacity to separate the language of feelings from that of his trade (even his earlier proposal was couched as 'filing a declaration').

Guppy is the first (and apart from Mr Turveydrop) the only person in the novel whose feelings towards Esther are changed radically by her disfigurement. Of course, he means well. The marvellous sentence 'My mother, though highly exasperating to the feelings, is actuated by maternal dictates' is touching as well as comic. His body language, throughout, shows acute embarrassment at his own behaviour: he has just enough self-awareness to know he is behaving badly. He apologises honourably for misconstruing Esther's motives for visiting (i.e. he fears she has come to hold him to his proposal) and he renews that proposal at a later date. But the damage is done. Later, having retrieved himself partly by promising to desist in his enquiries about Esther's past he is still so terrified that Esther might hold him to marriage that he pursues her down the street. He begs Esther – because 'it might be a satisfaction to your mind' – to repeat her admissions with Caddy as a witness. He is right about one thing: any renewal of his proposal ought to be out of the question: as he pleads at the end of the chapter, 'It couldn't be. Now could it, you know! I only put it to you'.

Compared with Texts 1 and 2, Esther's narration in this scene is almost without style. The language seems transparent: she simply records what people say and what they do. The comedy lies in the fact that what Guppy does is full of cliché: 'Mr Guppy said that any friend of mine was more than welcome'; 'Mr Guppy acknowledged its receipt by taking it out of his pocket, putting it to his lips …'. Curiously, however, Esther perceives the identity between mother and son, though without calling attention to this perception. The silent comedy of Mrs Guppy's 'jocoseness' arises from simply cataloguing her gestures: 'she rolled her head, and shook it, and put her handkerchief to her mouth, and appealed to Caddy with her elbow, and her hand'. Guppy's embarrassment is rendered in the same, almost clinical, listing: 'He put his hand [to his throat], coughed, made faces, tried again to swallow it, coughed again, made faces again, looked all round the room, and fluttered his papers.' Esher's own dignity of character, and perhaps also her likeness to her own mother, comes out in the simple directness of her own responses to his confused and panic-ridden speech: ' "There can be no doubt," said I, "that I declined your proposal without any. reservation or qualification whatever, Mr Guppy." ' At this stage in the novel, two chapters after her meeting her mother and the emotional assurance provided by Ada's acceptance of her new face, Esther is utterly self-possessed.

PART FIVE

BACKGROUND

CHARLES DICKENS'S LIFE & WORKS

Dickens was born in Portsmouth on 7 February 1812, the second of eight children. and was brought up mainly in the naval ports of Portsmouth and Chatham. His father John Dickens, was a naval clerk, and so prone to debt that he became the model of Mr Micawber in the autobiographical novel *David Copperfield* (always waiting 'for something to turn up'). When the family left Chatham in 1823 they were in debt, and Dickens was sent to work in a blacking factory, while his father was sent to the Marshalsea Debtor's Prison – vividly depicted in the novel *Little Dorrit*. When his father saw a chance for Dickens to be liberated from this humiliating work, so that he could pursue his education, his mother was indifferent: 'I never shall forget, I never can forget', said Dickens, 'that my mother was warm for my being sent back'.

In 1827 he took his first proper job, as an office boy with a firm of solicitors in Holborn, and then, having learned shorthand, became a freelance reporter, and wrote for such papers as *The Mirror of Parliament* and the *Morning Chronicle*. In 1829 he fell in love with Maria Beadnell, a banker's daughter, whom he loved tormentedly for years and ultimately immortalised as Estella in *Great Expectations* and Flora in *Little Dorrit*. This relationship continued on and off until, in 1836, he married Catherine Hogarth, the daughter of a fellow journalist.

In the year of his marriage, Dickens published his first book, *Sketches by Boz*, illustrated by George Cruikshank. His next project was the *Pickwick Papers* (1836–7), a set of sporting sketches illustrated by Hablôt Browne (Phiz), whose collaboration with Dickens went on until *Bleak House*. The success of *Pickwick Papers* and of the characters of Pickwick and Sam Weller, encouraged him to embark on two novels, *Oliver Twist* (1838) and *Nicholas Nickleby* (1839). Literary success brought him into contact with such celebrities as Leigh Hunt and Walter Savage Landor (on whom he based Skimpole and Boythorn in *Bleak House*). After a further two novels he was famous enough to make his first American tour in 1842, where he stirred up controversy over American disregard of copyright. One fruit of this tour was that he makes his leading character in *Martin Chuzzlewit* visit America, and experience a disillusionment with the profit-driven republic similar to his own.

Before the American tour Dickens's novels were prone to lurch from incident to incident and to be carried by (and carried away by) their characters: the most memorable facet of *Martin Chuzzlewit*, for instance, is the monstrous and inebriated nurse Mrs Gamp. After the American tour Dickens's novels became darker in tone, and more unified in theme. Between 1846 and 1850 he edited the *Daily News*, wrote the carefully plotted *Dombey and Son* (1848), with its picture of London as a great maw devouring an inward-streaming populace, and the autobiographical novel *David Copperfield* (1849–50) which fictionalises his own childhood.

His greatest novels coincide with the production of his two successive weekly magazines, *Household Words* and *All the Year Round*. In the first of these weeklies, which carried amusing and often trenchant investigative journalism, on such matters as class, women's education, poverty and industrial conditions, Dickens also serialised such major work as his own novel, *Hard Times*, his very republican version of English history, *A Child's History of England*, and much of the writing of Mrs Gaskell, including her novel *North and South*.

Bleak House (1852–3) was one of Dickens's most creative moments. In it he opened up a much darker seam of writing, and all the five major novels that follow *Bleak House* can be seen as developing some aspect of its technique. For instance, *Hard Times* (1854) is both an industrial novel, inspired by Gaskell's *Mary Barton* (1848), and a critique of the Utilitarian philosophy of Jeremy Bentham. According to Bentham himself:

> By the principle of utility is meant that principle which approves or disapproves of every action whatsoever, according to the tendency which it appears to have to augment or diminish the happiness of the party whose interest is in question.

In *Bleak House*, Grandfather Smallweed and the great principle of British law are part of Dickens's vigorous onslaught upon this principle of the calculation of self-interest. *Hard Times* compresses into a parable this aspect of *Bleak House* which is about people weighing each other up. In *Hard Times* a brutal, indifferent and materialist culture is attributed to an education system which has no room for the affections or the imagination, the two cardinal strengths of a Romantic vision of life, and therefore creates selfish and heartless people incapable of a moral life.

Little Dorrit (1855–7) pursues Dickens's attack on government, and on feckless and parasitical parents. *A Tale of Two Cities* (1859) fictionalises the horrors of the French Revolution, as if to remind his audience of the horrors of the sort of revolutionary violence with which England is **symbolically** threatened in *Bleak House*. In *Great Expectations* (1860–1) Dickens develops what he learnt from Esther about first-person narration. Pip, like Esther, is both a narrator and a character trying to piece together an identity. In this novel, also, he deepens the study of ambiguity that he began in Bucket, in the deeply ambivalent character of the lawyer Jaggers.

Our Mutual Friend (1865), his last complete novel, develops his symbolic method, his critique of capitalism, and his use of the grotesque. Its opening scene is set on the river, where a human scavenger skulls up and down looking for corpses to rob: this polluted river scene is developed throughout the novel in motifs of swamps, alligators and sharks. Dickens's treatment of people as inclined to merge with things also develops in *Our Mutual Friend*. The newly rich Veneerings are a bit sticky, like their furniture; and one of their friends, Twemlow, is introduced as if he *is* a piece of furniture: the reader may have some difficulty understanding that he is a person; but like Sir Leicester, he develops later. The grotesque qualities of characters like Krook and Smallweed are developed beautifully in the friendship between Silas Wegg, a man with a wooden leg, and Mr Venus, an articulator of human bones. As they converse in Mr Venus's shop, passing trains cause the skeletons and the babies in bottles to perform a macabre dance around them as they talk.

Dickens had separated from his wife in 1858, causing a considerable scandal, and indulged his infatuation for an actress Ellen Ternan – matters which naturally exercise the biographers. Throughout the 1860s he exhausted himself through intense and immensely popular public readings from his works – including such harrowing scenes as the murder of Nancy in *Oliver Twist* – and a second tour of the United States. Dickens died at Gad's Hill, Kent, on 9 June 1870, leaving the macabre *Mystery of Edwin Drood* unfinished.

When Dickens says in the preface to *Bleak House*, 'I have purposely dwelt upon the romantic side of familiar things' he seems to be referring to his romance exaggeration, and the use of such astonishing motifs as the spontaneous combustion of 'Chancellor' Krook. But Dickens was in more fundamental ways aligned with the Romantics. Blake's vision of London and Dickens's are much the same; both writers perceive massive systems of exploitation and disease: Blake's **symbolic** syphilis becomes Dickens's typhus. Dickens also shared with Blake and Wordsworth the Romantic cult of the child: *Bleak House*, like Dickens's other novels, presents no children with a safe, happy childhood – they tend to be orphaned, or psychologically abused, or victimised by monstrously selfish parents. One of the worst evils of Victorian society, as it appears in Dickens's novels, is the assassination of childhood. More fundamentally still, he shared with these poets a belief in what he called 'Fancy' and Wordsworth and Coleridge called 'Imagination'. The attentive reader will find in *Bleak House* and its notes innumerable **allusions** to the works of poets, especially the Romantic poets, Wordsworth, Coleridge and Byron.

But the major literary influence on Dickens was the Victorian 'prophet', Thomas Carlyle (1795–1881). Carlyle was born in the same year as the youngest of the Romantic poets, John Keats. Carlyle taught Dickens to distrust ideas of progress and purely material solutions to social problems. Above all he taught that merely structural changes in society could be of no value, except with a change of heart, and that only change in people can create new structures in society.

Carlyle developed four major themes in four major works. In *Sartor Resartus* he presented a fictional biography of an inspired philosopher whose life expresses a kind of secular conversion experience: a spiritual rebirth, *beyond religion*. His hero moves from nihilism to affirmation, or in Carlyle's terms from the 'Everlasting Nay', through the 'Centre of Indifference', to 'the Everlasting Yea'. Part of the 'Yea' is learning that life is a matter of perpetual development of the self, and this can only be done by work: your duty is to 'unfold yourself' and to do this you must find 'what thou canst work at'. Do not expect a blinding revelation as to what should be done, or make your humdrum circumstances an excuse for doing nothing: your circumstances are precisely the stuff out of which your destiny is to be made. Richard Clare, in *Bleak House*, is guilty of failing to understand this lesson – of which Esther is the embodiment.

In *Heroes and Hero-Worship* Carlyle preaches the necessity for great men (that is, 'able' men) to lead society out of its decay and give 'the herd' something to live for. Dickens's 'iron master' in *Bleak House* suggests that Dickens was remembering Carlyle's view that the future lay with industrialists, the new aristocrats, who had an heroic mission to fulfil if they could only be made aware of it. Mr Rouncewell is an unusually sympathetic representation of an industrialist, for Dickens, though in other novels Dickens is sympathetic to genuine inventors and entrepreneurs handicapped by bureaucrats, and **satirises** governmental red tape as the 'Circumlocution Office' in *Little Dorrit*.

In *Past and Present* and *Signs of the Times*, and in his great essay on 'Chartism', Carlyle diagnosed the ills of a society based purely on economic connections between man and man. The attack on what Carlyle called the 'cash nexus' is clearly a major theme of *Bleak House*. In *The French Revolution* (1837), of which John Stuart Mill said 'no greater work of genius, either historical or poetical, has been produced in this country for many years', Carlyle threatened England with a vision of the French Revolution as an uncompleted destiny which would fall upon the English middle class if they failed to find the will and vision for reform.

Carlyle not only provided Dickens with virtually all his ideas, he also influenced Dickens's **rhetoric** and symbolism. An amusing aspect of Carlyle's prophetic denunciations is his sardonic style of address to the age: his mocking of 'Your serene highnesses, your majesties' (in *Past and Present*) lies behind Dickens's rhetoric in dealing with the death of Jo. In *Signs of the Times* (1829) Carlyle described his age as above all 'a mechanical age'. This idea is reflected in Chapter 1 of *Bleak House*, where Dickens presents the image of lawyers as so many keys in a pianoforte, and is a motif of *Hard Times* where Dickens represents time as the 'great manufacturer' turning out characters on a production line. Carlyle said that 'British industrial existence seems fast becoming one huge poison *swamp* of reeking *pestilence*, physical and moral', an **image** which provides Dickens with symbols for *Our Mutual Friend* and *Bleak House*.

Most important, when considering Carlyle's influence on *Bleak House*, is that in *Past and Present* (in the chapter 'The Gospel of Mammonism') Carlyle uses the image of disease to focus social ills. He gives the example of an Irish Widow who appealed to her fellow creatures for relief and was refused:

The forlorn Irish widow appeals to her fellow creatures as if saying 'Behold I am sinking ...: I am your sister, *bone of your bone*; one God made us: ye must help me'. They answer, 'No. Impossible, thou art no sister of ours'.

When they produce *parchments* to prove their nonconnection, Carlyle comments:

Nothing is left but she prove her sisterhood by dying, and infecting you with *typhus*. Seventeen of you lying dead will not deny such proof that she was *flesh of your flesh*; and perhaps some of the living may lay it to heart.

Typhus, bone, flesh, parchments: all these are used to great effect in *Bleak House*.

DICKENS & HIS FICTIONAL CONTEMPORARIES

As a 'condition of England' novel, *Bleak House* is often classified with such lesser classics as Elizabeth Gaskell's *Mary Barton*, and *North and South*, Benjamin Disraeli's *Sybil: or, the Two Nations*, Charlotte Brontë's *Shirley*, George Eliot's *Felix Holt the Radical*, and Charles Kingsley's *Alton Locke*, and, of course, Dickens's own vivid sketch of industrialism in *Hard Times*.

In England, Dickens's great fictional contemporaries, apart from Elizabeth Gaskell (whom he admired) and Charlotte Brontë (whom he did not), included William Makepeace Thackeray, Wilkie Collins, George Gissing, George Meredith and George Eliot. Thackeray shares Dickens's talent for social **satire**, especially of wealth and snobbery, but little of his taste for the fantastic. Collins, in *The Moonstone* and *The Woman in White*, produced novels of mystery and detection which share some of Dickens's experimentalism. Gissing is more of a naturalist and much less prone to sentiment. George Meredith and George Eliot write, on the whole, far more soberly, making fewer concessions to a popular audience, and stay far more within the conventions of **realism**.

Purely in the context of English fiction, which at this date was dedicated to maximising realism – specialising in plausible characters, doing plausible things, from plausible motives in a plausible environment, which is recognisably an extension of our own world – Dickens's exuberance of style and willingness to combine the realistic and the fantastic, can make him seem the odd man out. This may be partly because his theory of the novel amounts to little more than exploiting the popular formula for the novel as summarised by Wilkie Collins, 'make 'em laugh, make 'em cry, make 'em wait'. But it may also be because he saw himself in a wider context than a purely English one. In America, his contemporaries include Washington Irving, the inventor of 'Rip Van Winkle', whose fictional sketches he imitated in *Pickwick Papers* and *Sketches by Boz*; Nathaniel Hawthorne, who shared Dickens's taste for romance, and anticipated his skill in manipulating cardboard characters in macabre and genuinely disturbing plots; Edgar Allan Poe, who pioneered the detective story and far exceeded Dickens in his taste for the macabre; and Herman Melville, whose masterpiece *Moby-Dick* is comparable to *Bleak House* as an anatomy of society, and exceeds even Dickens in its deployment of numerous experimental styles.

SOCIAL BACKGROUND

THE WOMAN QUESTION

Because *Bleak House* encompasses so many social themes, much has already been said in Part Three about the social and historical background. One aspect of the background needs a little fuller development. *Bleak House*, simply as a novel whose narration is shared between male and female voices, reflects an epoch of agitation on the woman question. In America, feminism was on the march (Dickens had observed the phenomenon of 'speechifying women' with some alarm when he visited back in 1842). At the Seneca Falls Convention of 1848, Lucretia Mott and Elizabeth Stady Canton published a 'Declaration of Sentiments' based on America's 'Declaration of Independence' (1776) and France's 'Declaration of the Rights of Man' (1789): 'The History of Mankind', they wrote, 'is a history of repeated injuries and usurpations on the part of man toward woman, having in direct object the establishment of an absolute tyranny over her.' Miss Wisk (briefly **satirised** in Chapter 30 for her views on woman and 'her tyrant Man') represents the Convention's radical position.

Michael Slater points out in *Dickens and Women* (Dent, 1983) that 'It was for Dickens a fundamental belief, as it was for the great majority of his contemporaries, that man's nature, his psychological and emotional make-up, differed, fundamentally and inherently, from woman's'. The operative phrase here, is 'as it was for the great majority of his contemporaries'. It was equally true, for instance, not only for the conservative Mrs Ellis and Queen Victoria, but also for such writers as Elizabeth Gaskell and George Eliot, such notable reformers as Florence Nightingale and Catherine Beecher, and for such liberal feminists as Barbara Bodichon, Maria Grey and Emily Shirreff.

The social consensus at this date is expressed in such remarks as these, all by women:

> Women, considered in their distinct and abstract nature, as isolated beings, must lose more than half their worth. They are, in fact, from their own constitution, and from the station they occupy in the world, strictly speaking, relative creatures. (Sarah Stickney Ellis, *The Women of England: their Social Duties and Domestic Habits*, 10th edn, 1839, p. 155)

> The wild and stupid theories advanced by a few women, of 'equal rights' and 'equal intelligence,' are not the opinions of their sex. I for one (with millions more) believe in the natural superiority of man, as I do in the existence of a God. (Caroline Norton, quoted in Jane G. Perkins, *Life of Mrs Norton*, Henry Holt, 1909, p. 150).

> If warmth of feeling, quickness of sympathy, ardour and generous devotion, are qualities we prize and love in the other sex, how painfully must their absence be felt in her whose mission on earth is to live for others (Maria Grey & Emily Shirreff, *Thoughts on Self-Culture Addressed to Women*, 1850, p. 324)

Caroline Norton, by the way, was a famous campaigner for women's property rights, and Dickens strongly supported her views on this issue. One could argue that Dickens's novel is highly critical of the first of these views, and that in constructing Esther as he does, he has regard to the sort of views expressed by Grey and Shirreff, who are treated with great respect in histories of feminism. Certainly, if Dickens thought that women were (ideally at least) tender and self-sacrificing, he was joined in that thought by such figures as Elizabeth Gaskell, George Eliot and Queen Victoria.

To think otherwise is to. enrol in a minority tradition, made up almost exclusively of Mary Wollstonecraft, whose *Vindication of the Rights of Women* (1792) denied that the mind had gender, a few Chartists and radical Unitarians who kept her views alive, and John Stuart Mill, whose *The Subjection of Women* (1869) is the major Victorian feminist classic. This minority tradition assumed that men and women were intellectually and morally equal and that any perceived difference was the result of socialisation – especially the exclusion of women from proper education and proper career opportunities. Other mid-century works, such as the immensely popular writings of Sarah Stickney Ellis, assumed that women were not only 'relative creatures' but intellectually inferior, properly confined to a domestic sphere, fit to deal only with the minor morals of life, where they should function as moral beacons, and otherwise programmed to obedience, submission and deference: 'As women, then, the first thing of importance is to be content to be inferior to men – inferior in mental power, in the same proportion that you are inferior in bodily strength' (*The Daughters of England: their Position in Society, Character and Responsibilities*, 1842, p. 11). Liberal feminists such as Grey and Shirreff argued that, while women were undoubtedly suited to caring roles, they might well express themselves in other fields, and it was nevertheless necessary for women to cultivate decisiveness and moral judgement (as Esther does): unfortunately, 'the complete dependence in which a young woman spends her youth ... is naturally unfavourable to the acquisition of judgement and decision' (*Thoughts on Self-Culture*).

While Dickens and John Stuart Mill are often thought to occupy opposite positions on the nature of women, and Mill fumed at 'that creature Dickens' for satirising public women in Mrs Jellyby and Mrs Pardiggle, there are several major theses in Mill's feminist classic that Dickens seems in sympathy with. Although this work appeared sixteen years after *Bleak House*, the ideas in it were common to the sort of circles Mill and Dickens moved in, and the gist of its arguments (co-authored by Harriet Taylor) appeared in an essay on 'Enfranchisement of Women', *Westminster Review*, July 1851, four months before Dickens started his novel.

You might like to ask yourself whether Dickens (on the evidence of his novels) would sympathise with any or all of the following extracts from *The Subjection of Women*, on legal equality, on domestic violence, on the nature of women, on women's employment, and on the attitudes of boys to their sisters and mothers:

- The principle which regulates the existing social relations between the two sexes – the legal subordination of one sex to the other – is wrong itself, and now one of the chief hindrances to human improvement; and … it ought to be replaced by a principle of perfect equality, admitting no power or privilege on the one side, nor disability on the other.

- In no other case (except that of a child) is the person who has been proved judicially to have suffered an injury, replaced under the physical power of the culprit who inflicted it. Accordingly wives, even in the most extreme and protracted cases of bodily ill-usage, hardly ever dare avail themselves of the laws made for their protection: and if, in a moment of irrepressible indignation, or by the interference of neighbours, they are induced to do so, their whole effort afterwards is to disclose as little as they can, and to beg off their tyrant from his merited chastisement.

- All women are brought up from the very earliest years in the belief that their ideal of character is the very opposite to that of men; not self will, and government by self-control, but submission, and yielding to the control of other. All the moralities tell them that it is the duty of women, and all the current sentimentalities that it is their nature, to live for others; to make complete abnegation of themselves, and to have no life but in their affections.

- What is now called the nature of women is an eminently artificial thing – the result of forced repression in some directions, unnatural stimulation in others. It may be asserted without scruple, that no other class of dependants have had their character so entirely distorted from its natural proportions by their relation with their masters …

- What women by nature cannot do, it is quite superfluous to forbid them from doing … the present bounties and protective duties in favour of men should be recalled.

- Well brought-up youths … are little aware, when a boy is differently brought up, how early the notion of his inherent superiority to a girl arises in his mind; how it grows with his growth and strengthens with his strength; how it is inoculated by one schoolboy upon another; how early the youth thinks himself superior to his mother, owing her perhaps forbearance, but no real respect; and how sublime and sultan-like a sense of superiority he feels, above all, over the woman whom he honours by admitting her to a partnership of his life.

No 'feminist' by modern criteria, Dickens nevertheless supported campaigns for women's property acts, campaigned against domestic violence, created characters who suggest that there is no clear divide between male and female traits, depicted numerous couples where the intelligence and aptitudes of the woman are clearly superior to those of the man, and specialised in brother-sister relationships, especially in *Hard Times* and *Our Mutual Friend*, where the sister's sacrifice of herself and her needs to those of a worthless brother are clearly meant to arouse the reader's ire.

Esther's and Ada's veneration of Jarndyce are not peculiar to Dickens, but part of the culture. This is Mrs Ellis, again, speaking of the privilege of sharing the life of a good man.

> With gratitude we ought to acknowledge our belief that morally and spiritually there is perfect equality between men and women [morals and spirituality aren't subject to scale!]; yet, in the character of a noble, enlightened, and truly good man, there is a power and a sublimity, so nearly approaching what we believe to be the nature and capacity of angels, that as no feeling can exceed, so no language can describe, the degree of admiration and respect which the contemplation of such a character must excite.

According to Mrs Ellis,

> to be permitted to dwell within the influence of such a man, *must* be a privilege of the highest order; to listen to his conversation, *must* be a perpetual feast; but to be admitted into his heart – to share his counsels, and to be the chosen companion of his joys and sorrows! – it is difficult to say whether humility or gratitude *should* preponderate in the feelings of the woman this distinguished and thus blest (*The Wives of England: their Relative Duties, Domestic Influence, and Social Obligations*, 1843, p. 65).

The striking thing is that although Esther does recognise that this is how she ought to feel, and in part does feel, her author has endowed her with other feelings that it is harmful to repress.

PART SIX

CRITICAL HISTORY &
BROADER PERSPECTIVES

RECEPTION

When *Bleak House* was published reviewers took it for granted that Dickens was, as *Bentley's Miscellany* put it, a writer who somehow contrives to captivate his readers while offending grossly against nature and breaking most of the rules of art. They looked for a humorous piece, notable mainly for its vivid daguerrotypes of character loosely connected into an episodic plot (the daguerrotype was invented by Daguerre in 1839 and Dickens's characters were frequently referred to as linguistic equivalents of portraits made by this early photographic process). Few expected, or found, any **symbolic** organisation, or any great skill in narrative technique, though they were alert to the range of social questions introduced and **satirised**. Many complained about the number of characters who had no discernible role in advancing the plot (the idea of characters as **metaphors** through which Dickens makes his major **thematic** statements was perhaps too radical an innovation). Many were disappointed by the absence, as they saw it, of genial humour, and most deplored a developing tendency toward exaggeration. Henry Crabb Robinson thought the fog exaggerated. The *Athenaeum* was shocked by the way Dickens exaggerated unfortunate human characteristics such as 'the hideous palsy of Grandfather Smallweed and the chattering idiocy of his wife'. G. H. Lewes thought Dickens wrong to encourage belief in such unscientific notions as spontaneous combustion. The *Illustrated London News* decided that the new novel confirmed another major weakness, an incapacity for constructing plot – 'No man, we are confident, could tell a story better if he had but a story to tell'. In Harold Skimpole, Mr Chadband, Mrs Jellyby and Mr Turveydrop, however, Dickens had added memorably to his and his readers' gallery of definitive types – literary characters useful as touchstones when categorising one's circle of acquaintance. There was general appreciation of the sweetness of character of Esther (though not of her role as narrator), the pathos of Jo, the geniality of Trooper George, and the triumphant creation of Inspector Bucket, but absolutely no sense that the range of characters in the novel were linked by thematic consistencies. If the novel had a purpose, it was assumed, it was not to diagnose the condition of England, or the soul of man under capitalism, or original sin, but simply to expose the infamies of Chancery practice (*Bentley's Monthly Review*, the *Eclectic Review*), or slander clergymen (two reviews objected to Mr Chadband on these grounds) or make uninformed criticism of the Constitution. 'An unrivalled humorist, and eminently respectable in his morals, his knowledge of human nature is as superficial as it is extensive': so Dickens was summed up in *The Rambler*, January 1854.

Nowadays, such responses seem to be missing the point, and missing major kinds of originality – especially in symbolic unity and **analogical** construction. When, at long last, the seriousness of Dickens was recognised, and his popularity no longer held against him (as it was until the 1950s), the earliest emphasis was on the detailed topicality of *Bleak House*, and its qualification to be considered, therefore, alongside other fiction offering an imaginative account of 'the condition of England'.

FURTHER READING

For the early reception see Philip Collins, ed., *Dickens: the Critical Heritage*, Routledge & Kegan Paul, 1971, and the 'Early Reviews and Comment' in A. E. Dyson, *Dickens: Bleak House*, Macmillan, 1960 (Casebook). For readings of the novel as an anatomy of England see Humphrey House, *The Dickens World*, OUP, 1941, together with two essays in Dyson's casebook, John Butt & Kathleen Tillotson, 'The Topicality of Bleak House' (from their *Dickens at Work*, 1957), and Edgar Johnson, 'The Anatomy of Society', from his *Charles Dickens: his Tragedy and Triumph*, 1953. For a broader overview of the political significance of the novel, see the fine chapter on *Bleak House* in John Lucas, *Charles Dickens: the Major Novels*, Penguin, 1992.

THE PROBLEM OF ESTHER

Since Q. D. Leavis and A. E. Dyson warned them off in major essays, critics have been less prone to agree with her 'godmother' that Esther had been 'better not born': they have come to value what Dyson in his terms and Leavis in hers, recognised as a considerable triumph of empathy and of style, infuriating precisely because of its success in conveying the damage of dependency, and the need for illegitimates in all walks of life, at all stages of their lives, even into comparatively recent times, to apologise constantly for their existence. Critics have come to view her sympathetically, as a young woman desperately confused about her identity, or plausibly apologetic for her illegitimate existence, or in search for a mother in whom to find her self. Naturally, feminist studies of *Bleak House* have focused on Esther. Suzanne Graver, for instance, sees Dickens as having combined two voices in Esther, 'a dominant one that is cheerfully accepting and selflessly accommodating; and a muted one, itself double-edged, that is inquiring, critical, and discontented but also hesitant, self-disparaging and defensive'. Laurie Langbauer sees Esther as 'Dickens's fullest representation of the inside of a woman's mind because it shows one so brainwashed by and intent on maintaining the male order'.

Critics have perceived, also, that a dual narrative which offers contrary world pictures or value systems (essentially, that things are irremediable or remediable, as in *Great Expectations*), and fails to resolve them, leaves the reader (as does *Great Expectations*) in a writerly role. Carol Senf has argued that this role is peculiarly set up so as to require the reader to synthesise, androgynously, starkly male and female perceptions. Certainly the novel has a male half and a female half; occupying as it were, different spheres, but given their shared values, clearly split from a single egg. As the novel approaches its conclusion, and narration alternates from chapter to chapter, the problem becomes more apparent. When the third-person narrative leads us to Esther's door, and Esther opens it and takes up the narrative of Bucket's search for Lady Dedlock, what difference do we register? There is considerable dissent, by the way, about the question as to whether the views of the two narrators are in fact polarised at all. Kate Flint finds that Esther has as much inconsistency, and is as inclusive, as the omniscient narrator. Although sometimes she is a gendered character this is only when her limitations are dominant. John Lucas, however, takes them to be representing very different value systems and insists on the strengths and uniqueness of Esther's perceptions, her challenge to male assumptions.

THE PROBLEM OF ESTHER continued

FURTHER READING

Q. D. Leavis, 'Bleak House: a Chancery World', in *Dickens: the Novelist*, Chatto & Windus, 1973; W. J. Harvey, '*Bleak House*: the Double Narrative' in Dyson, Casebook; A. E. Dyson, '*Bleak House*: Esther Better not Born?', in Dyson, Casebook; Suzanne Graver, 'Writing in a Womanly Way and the Double Vision of *Bleak House*', *Dickens Quarterly* 1, March 1987, pp. 1–14; Laurie Langbauer, *Women and Romance: the Consolations of Gender in the English Novel*, Cornell University Press, 1961, pp. 1–18; Carol A. Senf, '*Bleak House*: Dickens, Esther and the Androgynous Mind', *Victorian Newsletter*, 1983, pp. 21–7; John Lucas, as above; Kate Flint, *Dickens*, Harvester New Reading, Harvester Press, 1986.

FEMINIST APPROACHES

According to Donald Hall in *Fixing Patriarchy*, the battery of Merry in *Martin Chuzzlewit*, together with the bludgeoning of Mrs Joe, the battery of Estella, and the burning of Miss Havisham, all in *Great Expectations*, serve to remind women of what might be in store for them should they challenge the boundaries set for them by patriarchy. More psychological interpretations have seen Dickens's recurring archetype of a worthless brother taking for granted the self-sacrifice of an intellectually, morally and imaginatively superior sister, in *Hard Times* and *Our Mutual Friend*, as a device whereby Dickens reaps credit for overcoming, while actually revenging, his own childhood grievance about being sent to a blacking factory so that his sister could be cosseted and enjoy music lessons.

So, did Dickens punish Lady Dedlock by freezing her to death? Or does he, rather, place the respectable reader in the hands, for some 600 pages, of an illegitimate daughter, and make Sir Leicester Dedlock most fully human in the moment of his selfless regard for the 'fallen' mother (indeed promote him for the first time from a cipher into a man for that very purpose) in order to challenge such morality? Is Hortense arrested to remind women not to overstep the mark? Or are Tulkinghorn murdered and Krook combusted to warn men not to torment women or collect their hair in sacks? Arguing from plot events, in themselves, is probably futile, and such arguments may say more about the critic than the novelist.

Interestingly, Esther Summerson, gifted (by her mordantly humorous Aunt?) with a pointedly patronymic surname, 'Summerson', rather than the ungendered Barbary or the potentially derogatory hoyden/Hawdon) loses no opportunity to draw attention to the victimised woman as a staple of her society. The novel conducts a kind of dialectic, in which Esther's savage portrayal of Mrs Jellyby and Mrs Pardiggle represents the thesis (Ellen Moers calls this Dickens's 'immediate surface reaction' to the issue of women) and her subtler but equally savage portrayal of Skimpole and Turveydrop represent the antithesis; while the very structure of the novel suggests a binary synthesis, with Esther Summerson's intellectual development as one half of that synthesis, and the omniscient narrator's enlarging sympathies as the other half.

Brenda Ayres, Ellen Moers and other feminist critics have pointed out that this novel does much to undermine the view that women should confine themselves to a domestic sphere. Had Esther, or Mrs Bagnet, or Mrs Rouncewell, or Mrs Bucket stayed at home the novel's few conclusive events would not have occurred. Esther, Ellen Moers has said, is a fictionalised version of Dickens's friend and correspondent, the philanthropic Angela Burdett-Coutts, and portrayed as the necessary director of Jarndyce's charitable energies; Mrs Bagnet, like Caddy, is not merely a homemaker but an entrepreneur, successful proprietress of a musical instruments shop; Mrs Rouncewell, moreover, is a prototype of the professional housekeeper, and one who is quite prepared to put the rescue of her son before the interests of the Dedlock family; Mrs Bucket, we are told, has all the aptitude of a professional detective. All four – like the decisive Lady Dedlock in adventurous pursuit of her lover's resting place – are prone to make decisive interventions involving independent excursions. Even the notoriously passive Ada sets up house with Richard on her own initiative, in defiance of Jarndyce's prohibition. A contrary view has been expressed by Virginia Blain, who argues that the novel covertly fosters violence against women, which is appeased only by the death of Lady Dedlock (after a pursuit which is meant to save but 'in fact' hastened her death), and that Esther can only survive by colluding with patriarchy, joining with Bucket in hunting her mother down. She is rewarded for 'having purged her mother's sexual taint' and conniving in 'her own clitoridectomy'.

FURTHER READING

Donald E. Hall, *Fixing Patriarchy: Feminism and Mid-Victorian Male Novelists*, Macmillan, 1996; Brenda Ayres, *Dissenting Women: the Subversion of Domestic Ideology*, Greenwood Press, 1998; Ellen Moers, '*Bleak House*: the Agitating Women', *The Dickensian*, 1973, pp. 13–24; Richard Gravil, 'The Androgyny of Bleak House', *Master Narratives: Tellers and Telling in the English Novel*, Ashgate Press, 2001; Virginia Blain, 'Double Vision and the Double Standard in *Bleak House*: A Feminist Perspective' in Jeremy Tambling's New Casebook, *Bleak House*, Macmillan, 1998.

PSYCHOLOGICAL APPROACHES

Dickens, nowadays, is thought to be deeper and subtler than people used to think. The psyche of Esther does not come out only in what she says about herself – though this can sometimes be trusted – but in her gestures, her habit of gazing in the mirror, her way of addressing herself in the third person, her fever-ridden nightmare, her self-interruptions and evasions. She is, quite clearly, intent from the start on erasing from her personality all personal desire; yet as Brenda Ayres points out, these desires will not (like her doll) stay buried, and remain too close to the surface not to be felt in all instances where a passional self is in question. In burying her doll she may be burying her natural self, or her desires, or her selfishness in wanting a mother. Her anxious consulting of mirrors implies to critics brought up on the psychology of D. W. Winnicott that since a baby's first 'mirror' is the mother's face Esther has to seek for a mother before she can develop a healthy self-image. Since constant nicknames imperil her already fragile identity, she constantly looks into the mirror to reclaim herself. Unfortunately, on the other side of the mirror is a mother who has veiled her own identity and who, when she looks into her own mirror in one scene, sees not herself but Hortense. Alex Zwerdling, in a sympathetic account of Dickens's creation, sees Esther as 'alienated from her true self and unable to acknowledge her deepest feelings' and the character as 'Dickens's most ambitious attempt to allow a character who does not fully understand herself to tell her own story'.

FURTHER READING
Lawrence Frank, 'Through a Glass darkly: Esther Summerson and *Bleak House*', *Dickens Studies Annual*, 4, 1975, pp. 97–112, and Albert D. Hutter, ' "The High Tower of His Mind": Psychoanalysis and *Bleak House*', *Criticism* 19, 1977, pp. 296–316, both reprinted in *Critical Essays on Charles Dickens Bleak House*, ed. Eliot L. Gilbert, G.K. Hall, 1989, pp. 64–83; Alex Zwerdling, 'Esther Summerson Rehabilitated', in *Charles Dickens: New Perspectives*, ed. Wendell Stacy Johnson, Prentice-Hall, 1982, pp. 94–113. Two essays in Tambling's New Casebook which make some use of the theories of Freud and Lacan are Christine Boheemen-Saaf, ' "The Universe Makes an Indifferent Parent": *Bleak House* and the Victorian Family Romance', 1983, and Timothy Peltason, 'Esther's Will', 1991.

Deconstruction

Deconstruction derives from the work of a French philosopher, Jacques Derrida. Derrida's thinking is developed from the now commonplace notion of the arbitrariness of linguistic signs. Words have no necessary relation to things, and can only have meaning through their difference from other signs – so the meaning of any statement is dependent on its relation to the surrounding system of language. Deconstruction revels in the idea that meaning is illusory, and that texts inevitably deconstruct themselves because of the indeterminancy in language itself.

The most famous modern essay on this novel is J. Hillis Miller's mildly deconstructive 'Interpretation in Bleak House' which argues that the work is itself about language, signs and interpretation. I say 'mildly' because Miller starts by conceding that *Bleak House* 'accurately reflects the social reality of Dickens's day' and constructs 'a model in little of English society in his time', then describes the novel as 'an imitation in words of the culture of a city'. Only then does he develop a brilliant series of observations concerning the fictiveness of Dickens's fiction, its self-referentiality. Miller sees what Victorian critics could not see, that **metaphor** and **metonymy** make up the 'grammatical armature' of the novel. Each character is **analogous** to other characters, and to be understood only by their reference to and difference from other characters. Similarly, things, such as fog and the law, Krook's shop and Chancery, are understood in terms of one another. Numerous characters have only a linguistic existence, and even named characters tend to have openly or covertly metaphorical names inviting us to interpret and thus reify them – their names usurping their 'reality'. The alphabetical series of endlessly substitutable Boodles, Coodles, Doodles, Buffys, Cuffys, Duffys, implies interchangeability. Even Esther can see herself as just a bead on a necklace of fire, and everyone (except perhaps the lawyers) is ultimately one of a series of victims. You may like to think about Miller's argument that the novel is basically about 'the sign-making power itself', or language as violence, or naming as possession. Is this just a fashionable piece of critical Dandyism? Or is the novel 'really' about how we are all trapped in systems of appropriation, as a kind of original sin? It may even imply that all systems of interpretation are equally liable to error. Esther, with her sense of duty, may seem to represent a moral centre, but what she stands for is deconstructed by the presence in her own narrative of her negation, Skimpole – someone who simply refuses to be defined by social responsibilities. Intriguingly, Skimpole, who was for some Victorian critics wholly extraneous to the novel's plot or significance, has become for some deconstructive critics almost the central character.

Jeremy Tambling's New Casebook includes other readings which exemplify Derrida's basic stance that any meaning we give to a text is 'haunted' by other and perhaps opposite meanings. D. A. Miller, for instance, reads *Bleak House* through Michel Foucault rather than Derrida. Foucault analyses nineteenth-century society through images of discipline, control and surveillance, in such books as *Discipline and Punish* and *The History of Sexuality*. D. A. Miller sees *Bleak House* as centred on the law as a system of control. Its central character is Bucket, who (in Jeremy Tambling's words) 'symbolises a new type of surveillance' and 'a wish to find out people's secrets and expose them, drive them out, or normalise them'. The novel's overall ambivalence is focused in its ambivalent representation of Bucket as decent family man, devoted to private attachments, and amoral public enforcer. So the very qualities of *Bleak House* that worried its Victorian critics – irresponsible exaggeration, self-generating flights of verbal invention, externally observed characters, unreality, failures of plot, inconclusiveness, pessimism – are transfigured in much modern criticism into the novel's primary virtues, tokens of its scepticism about the knowability of persons and things, and its radical modernity.

FURTHER READING

J. Hillis Miller, Introduction, *Bleak House*, Penguin 1971 (also available as an essay in Tambling). See also, in Jeremy Tambling's New Casebook, his own authoritative 'Introduction', and two essays in the collection: D. A. Miller, 'Discipline in Different Voices: Bureaucracy, Police, Family and *Bleak House*', 1988, and Dominick LaCapra, 'Ideology and Critique in Dickens's *Bleak House*', 1984.

SELECTED FURTHER READING

Peter Ackroyd, *Dickens*, Sinclair-Stevenson, 1990; Minerva, 1991
 A recent biography

Edgar Johnson, *Charles Dickens: His Tragedy and Triumph*, 2 vols, Gollancz, 1953
 The standard biography

Susan Shatto, ed. *The Companion to Bleak House*, Allen & Unwin, 1988
 Invaluable on Dickens's sources

Three excellent mainstream critical studies not mentioned above are:

F. R. & Q. D. Leavis, *Dickens the Novelist*, Chatto & Windus, 1970; Penguin Books, 1972

John Lucas, *The Melancholy Man: a Study of Dickens's Novels*, Methuen, 1970

J. Hillis Miller, *Charles Dickens: The World of His Novels*, Harvard University Press, 1958

Historical events	Dickens's life	Cultural events
		1811 William Makepeace Thackeray born
1812 Napoleon's retreat from Moscow	**1812** Charles John Huffam Dickens born Portsmouth	
		1813 Jane Austen, *Sense and Sensibility*
1815 Battle of Waterloo		
	1816 Family moves to Chatham	
		1818 Mary Shelley, *Frankenstein*
		1819 'George Eliot' born
1820 Death of George III; first gas lighting in cities		
		1821 John Keats dies; Feodor Dostoevski born
	1822 Family moves to London	
1824 Trade Unions officially allowed	**1824** Father imprisoned for debt; Dickens works in shoe-blacking factory	
	1824-7 At school at Wellington House Academy	
1825 First railway Stockton-Darlington		
1826 First Atlantic crossing under steam		
		1827 William Blake dies, Beethoven dies
	1829 Falls in love with Maria Beadnell	**1829** Thomas Carlyle, *Signs of the Times*
		1831 Victor Hugo, *The Hunchback of Notre-Dame*
1832 Reform Bill passed	**1832** Becomes reporter of debates in House of Commons	**1832** Walter Scott dies; Goethe dies; Jeremy Bentham dies

Historical events	Dickens's life	Cultural events
1833 First British Factory Act		**1833** Carlyle, *Sartor Sartorus*
		1832-4 Harriet Martineau, *Illustrations of Political Economy*
1834 Tolpuddle Martyrs; first electric light	**1834** Becomes reporter on *Morning Chronicle*	
		1835 Benjamin Disraeli, *Sybil*
1836 People's Charter	**1836** Meets John Forster, friend, adviser and biographer	
	1836-7 *Sketches by Boz; The Posthumous Papers of the Pickwick Club;* marries Catherine Hogarth	
1837 Accession of Queen Victoria	**1837-8** *Oliver Twist*	**1837** Thomas Carlyle, *The French Revolution*
1838 First photographic prints	**1838-9** *Nicholas Nickleby*	
1839 First electric telegraph in use on railways		
	1840-1 *The Old Curiosity Shop*	**1840** Thomas Hardy and Emile Zola born
1841 London-Bristol railway opened; hundreds of new railway lines constructed during next decade	**1841** *Barnaby Rudge*	
1842 Edwin Chadwick, *Inquiry into the Sanitary Condition of the Labouring Population of Great Britain*	**1842** Visits America	**1842** Sarah Stickney Ellis, *The Daughters of England*
	1843-4 *Martin Chuzzlewit*	**1843** Thomas Carlyle's *Past and Present* attacks laissez-faire economics and arouses sympathy for industrial poor; Sarah Stickney Ellis, *The Wives of England*

Historical events	Dickens's life	Cultural events
	1844 Visits Italy	
	1845 *A Christmas Carol*	
	1846 Founds *Daily News;* visits Switzerland	
1847 Burdett-Coutts founds home for Homeless Women	**1847** Helps set up home for Homeless Women	**1847** Emily Brontë, *Wuthering Heights;* Charlotte Brontë, *Jane Eyre;* Anne Brontë, *Agnes Grey*
1848 Revolutions in Paris, Berlin, Vienna, Venice, Rome, Milan, Prague and Budapest	**1848** *Dombey and Son*	**1848** Elizabeth Gaskell, *Mary Barton;* Thackeray, *Vanity Fair;* Karl Marx, *Communist Manifesto*
	1849-50 *David Copperfield*	
1850 First refrigerator; John Simon, *Report on the Sanitary Condition of the City*	**1850** Starts *Household Words*	**1850** Guy de Maupassant born; Tennyson becomes Poet Laureate; Nathaniel Hawthorne, *The Scarlet Letter;* Wordsworth and Balzac die
	1850-2 *Bleak House*	
1851 Great Exhibition; gold discovered in Australia	**1851-3** *A Child's History of England*	**1851** The painter Turner dies; Henry Mayhew, *London Labour and London Poor;* Herman Melville, *Moby Dick*
1852 First airship		
1853 Chloroform given medical approval		
1853-4 Cotton worker's strike, Preston		
1853-6 Crimean War		
	1854 Visits Preston; *Hard Times*	
	1855-7 *Little Dorrit*	**1855** Elizabeth Gaskell, *North and South;* Charlotte Brontë dies

Historical events	Dickens's life	Cultural events
1857 Indian Mutiny		**1857** Gustave Flaubert, *Madame Bovary*
	1858 Separates from wife; in love with Ellen Ternan	
	1859 *A Tale of Two Cities*	**1859** Charles Darwin, *On the Origin of Species;* George Eliot, *Adam Bede*
	1860 Moves to Gad's Hill, near Rochester	
	1860-1 *Great Expectations*	
1861 First telephone		
		1862 Victor Hugo, *Les Misérables;*
	1863 Son Walter dies in India	**1863** Thackeray dies; Charles Kingsley, *The Water-Babies;* Caroline Norton, *Lost and Saved*
	1864-5 *Our Mutual Friend*	
		1866 George Eliot, *Felix Holt the Radical*
	1867-8 Revisits America	
1868 First bicycle (bone-shaker)		**1868** Wilkie Collins, *The Moonstone*
		1869 Leo Tolstoy, *War and Peace* John Stuart Mill, *On the Subjection of Women*
1870 Education Act; all children to have elementary education	**1870** Dies; *The Mystery of Edwin Drood* unfinished	
		1871-2 George Eliot, *Middlemarch*
	1872-4 John Forster's *Life of Dickens*	

allegory a story or picture in which the characters or events are designed to stand in for a concealed level of meaning. Dickens makes fun of antiquarian 'Allegory in a Roman Helmet' but uses it himself. For instance, the accumulation of debris in Krook's shop allegorises the disorder of Chancery proceedings

alliteration a sequence of matching consonants at the beginning of words or stressed syllables

allusion a passing reference in a work of literature to something outside itself, whether another literary text, or to legends, historical events and personages

analogy a word, or thing, used for purposes of comparison or contrast. Numerous novels make use of what a critic once called 'the analogical matrix', and in *Bleak House*, persistent analogies between characters and their actions are a major part of the technique

anaphora (Gk, 'carrying back, repetition') the name for repetition in successive clauses of a word or phrase. Dickens uses this effect repeatedly in descriptive and narrative passages

assonance the correspondence in two words or more of stresses vowel sounds

Deconstruction a critical fashion founded on the gap between signifier (words) and signified (what words refer to). Extreme deconstructionists may deny that texts can ever refer reliably to anything outside themselves. Deconstructive readings tend to replace the search for definitive meaning with the generation of an infinite series of undecidable possibilities

distance a term describing the detachment of the author from what is being said, or the character saying it. Rapid variation in 'distance' between author and speaker is an essential component of irony

doubles characters whose relationship seems to be psychological, in that they function less as independent characters than as the expression of something repressed in a major character. Thus Gridley and Hortense may be seen not as the opposites of the mild Jarndyce and Esther but as their vengeful, out-of-control, doubles

euphemism a mild or evasive expression substituted for a blunt one

feminist criticism a set of critical approaches, which when applied to male writing seeks to expose the complicity of literary texts with structures of gender oppression, for instance in the marginalisation or denigration of women, or the employment of language which takes the male to be standard, the female as 'other'

genre a type or division of literature. Poetry, drama and prose fiction are the primary literary genres; but each is divisible into further genres. *Bleak House* is a novel, but might also be related to the detective novel, the *bildungsroman*, prose satire, and so forth

heptameter a line of seven feet in English verse

hyperbole use of exaggerated language. A constant feature of irony; whenever a character in Bleak House praises the system we may suspect hyperbole

iambic pentameter a poetic line of five iambic feet (in iambic meter an unstressed syllable precedes each stressed one)

image/ imagery a hopelessly ambiguous term, covering anything from word-pictures of concrete things (mud, fog, ink), or more general ones (gloom, decay, desperation) to figures of speech such as simile, metaphor, personification

invective the denunciation of someone or something in a brief or sustained outburst of derogatory or vituperative language. It tends to come into play whenever Dickens, or Jarndyce or Gridley have lawyers in view

irony (Gk. 'dissembling') a manner of speaking or writing which exploits the gap between what is said and what is meant. In Greek comedy the 'Eiron' pretended to be stupid and naïve, while his antagonist, the Alazon, was complacent and boastful. What the Eiron said was understated, its meaning concealed. In fiction, irony exploits the unreliable narrator: we have to work out whether the speaker's perceptions or judgements are to be trusted. The speaker may be quite unironic, as Esther sometimes seems to be, when used as a mask for the author's ironic intent

metaphor the expression of one thing in terms of another: love, Shakespeare claims, in one of his less reliable moments, is 'the star to every wandering bark'. That is, it is so fixed and unchanging that you can navigate by it. Metaphor can be implied. When the barristers in Chapter 1 are 'floundering' in precedents the law is compared to mud

metonymy the substitution of the name of some entity, such as a barrister, or monarchy, by something associated with it, i.e. silk or crown. *Bleak House* works through insistent metonymy in that such individual images as wheels, mud, whips, ink, parchment, mace, are also metonymies for carriages, decay, angry travellers, writing, documents, authority. Even the characters in this novel tend to be metonymic of classes (Jo represents an entire under-class; Mrs Pardiggle the whole problem of 'rapacious benevolence') and social relations

narrator the teller of a story, or a history. Fictional narrators range from the omniscient (who knows everything) to the dysfunctional, and may be dramatised or undramatised. At one end of the scale there may be an impersonal narrator whom we are likely to trust, if only because we have no other viewpoint within the story; at the other a dramatically involved narrator who may be ignorant of some events, prejudiced, or incapable of understanding what is happening. In *Bleak House* the two narrators may, at first, seem to occupy these two extremes

onomatopoeia the use of words whose sounds imitate the objects or actions described (e.g. cuckoo, scratch)

oxymoron a figure of speech in which contradictory terms are brought together in what seems like an impossible combination

parody an imitation of a work of literature devised to ridicule its special characteristics

pastiche a work of art made up of fragments of an original

periphrasis circumlocution, designed for elegant variation, or for humorous effect

point of view in fiction this does not mean 'opinion', but the perspective from which the narrative is offered. See narrator. Although one narrator in this novel is usually considered omniscient, 'he' clearly chooses to conceal a number of matters from the reader, as, in a different way, does Esther, who appears for much of the novel as an innocent eye but knows considerably more than she chooses to reveal

psychological criticism some psychological critics approach the work of art as the expression of the author's personality, perhaps shaped by unconscious drives and symbolising, involuntarily, what is repressed in the writer's conscious mind; others simply interpret literary texts by applying the insights of such authorities as Jung, Fred, Winnicott, Lacan

realism as a literary mode, is desirous of creating a faithful picture of reality (or the illusion of reality). It tends to be associated, also, with the desire to project a moral view of life, mainly because realism, originally, meant a preoccupation with the 'real' world of ideas, rather than the world of appearances

reportage a style of writing based upon compressed report of dialogue or incident frequently using a form of shorthand, such as including only one side of a dialogue, as in the report of Jo's interrogation at 'the Inkwich'

rhetoric speech or writing of unusual formality, or heightened quality, designed to persuade, move or impress; sometimes associated with insincerity

satire literature which exhibits or examines vice and folly (or simply ideas or values the writer does not agree with) and makes them appear ridiculous or contemptible

simile a figure of speech comparing one thing with another, using 'like' or 'as'

symbolism some of the abundant imagery in *Bleak House* is clearly metaphorical or metonymic, in that Dickens is referring to something else through the image. Some of it, however, through frequent usage, seems to carry a much broader and less specific, or thematic, connotation, pointing towards a universal meaning. 'Fog' is a meteorological image, a fact of London life, and a metaphor for the obfuscation caused by the law; but more than that it seems to symbolise the human condition. 'Sheepskin' is not only the raw material out of which parchment is made, but from its nauseous recurrence in the novel, a symbol expressive of how life is converted into property. A pair of frayed slippers can be simply an image; but in *Bleak House* they symbolise entropy

theme a central idea in a work, such as, in this case, reification, control, exploitation, cruelty, avarice, detection

Utilitarianism a philosophy founded by Jeremy Bentham which argued that all things can be settled by appeal to 'the greatest good of the greatest number' but which Dickens saw as encouraging the replacement of benevolence by calculation and self-interest

Author of this note

Richard Gravil's recent publications include *Romantic Dialogues: Anglo-American Continuities, 1776–1862* (St Martin's Press, 2000), *Master Narratives: Tellers and Telling in the English Novel* (Ashgate, 2001) and two other titles in this series, *Jonathan Swift: Gulliver's Travels and a Modest Proposal*, and *Samuel Taylor Coleridge: Selected Poems*.

York Notes Advanced (£3.99 each)

Margaret Atwood
Cat's Eye

Margaret Atwood
The Handmaid's Tale

Jane Austen
Mansfield Park

Jane Austen
Persuasion

Jane Austen
Pride and Prejudice

Alan Bennett
Talking Heads

William Blake
Songs of Innocence and of Experience

Charlotte Brontë
Jane Eyre

Emily Brontë
Wuthering Heights

Angela Carter
Nights at the Circus

Geoffrey Chaucer
The Franklin's Prologue and Tale

Geoffrey Chaucer
The Miller's Prologue and Tale

Geoffrey Chaucer
Prologue To the Canterbury Tales

Geoffrey Chaucer
The Wife of Bath's Prologue and Tale

Samuel Taylor Coleridge
Selected Poems

Joseph Conrad
Heart of Darkness

Daniel Defoe
Moll Flanders

Charles Dickens
Great Expectations

Charles Dickens
Hard Times

Emily Dickinson
Selected Poems

John Donne
Selected Poems

Carol Ann Duffy
Selected Poems

George Eliot
Middlemarch

George Eliot
The Mill on the Floss

T.S. Eliot
Selected Poems

F. Scott Fitzgerald
The Great Gatsby

E.M. Forster
A Passage to India

Brian Friel
Translations

Thomas Hardy
The Mayor of Casterbridge

Thomas Hardy
The Return of the Native

Thomas Hardy
Selected Poems

Thomas Hardy
Tess of the d'Urbervilles

Seamus Heaney
Selected Poems from Opened Ground

Nathaniel Hawthorne
The Scarlet Letter

Kazuo Ishiguro
The Remains of the Day

Ben Jonson
The Alchemist

James Joyce
Dubliners

John Keats
Selected Poems

Christopher Marlowe
Doctor Faustus

Arthur Miller
Death of a Salesman

John Milton
Paradise Lost Books I & II

Toni Morrison
Beloved

Sylvia Plath
Selected Poems

Alexander Pope
Rape of the Lock and other poems

William Shakespeare
Antony and Cleopatra

William Shakespeare
As You Like It

William Shakespeare
Hamlet

William Shakespeare
King Lear

William Shakespeare
Measure for Measure

William Shakespeare
The Merchant of Venice

William Shakespeare
A Midsummer Night's Dream

William Shakespeare
Much Ado About Nothing

William Shakespeare
Othello

William Shakespeare
Richard II

William Shakespeare
Romeo and Juliet

William Shakespeare
The Taming of the Shrew

William Shakespeare
The Tempest

William Shakespeare
Twelfth Night

William Shakespeare
The Winter's Tale

George Bernard Shaw
Saint Joan

Mary Shelley
Frankenstein

Jonathan Swift
Gulliver's Travels and A Modest Proposal

Alfred, Lord Tennyson
Selected Poems

Alice Walker
The Color Purple

Oscar Wilde
The Importance of Being Earnest

Tennessee Williams
A Streetcar Named Desire

John Webster
The Duchess of Malfi

Virginia Woolf
To the Lighthouse

W.B. Yeats
Selected Poems

Jane Austen
Emma

Jane Austen
Sense and Sensibility

Samuel Beckett
Waiting for Godot and
Endgame

Louis de Bernières
Captain Corelli's Mandolin

Charlotte Brontë
Villette

Caryl Churchill
Top Girls and *Cloud Nine*

Charles Dickens
Bleak House

T.S. Eliot
The Waste Land

Thomas Hardy
Jude the Obscure

Homer
The Iliad

Homer
The Odyssey

Aldous Huxley
Brave New World

D.H. Lawrence
Selected Poems

Christopher Marlowe
Edward II

George Orwell
Nineteen Eighty-four

Jean Rhys
Wide Sargasso Sea

William Shakespeare
Henry IV Pt I

William Shakespeare
Henry IV Part II

William Shakespeare
Macbeth

William Shakespeare
Richard III

Tom Stoppard
Arcadia and *Rosencrantz and
Guildenstern are Dead*

Virgil
The Aeneid

Jeanette Winterson
*Oranges are Not the Only
Fruit*

Tennessee Williams
Cat on a Hot Tin Roof

Metaphysical Poets

GCSE and equivalent levels (£3.50 each)

Maya Angelou
I Know Why the Caged Bird Sings

Jane Austen
Pride and Prejudice

Alan Ayckbourn
Absent Friends

Elizabeth Barrett Browning
Selected Poems

Robert Bolt
A Man for All Seasons

Harold Brighouse
Hobson's Choice

Charlotte Brontë
Jane Eyre

Emily Brontë
Wuthering Heights

Shelagh Delaney
A Taste of Honey

Charles Dickens
David Copperfield

Charles Dickens
Great Expectations

Charles Dickens
Hard Times

Charles Dickens
Oliver Twist

Roddy Doyle
Paddy Clarke Ha Ha Ha

George Eliot
Silas Marner

George Eliot
The Mill on the Floss

Anne Frank
The Diary of Anne Frank

William Golding
Lord of the Flies

Oliver Goldsmith
She Stoops To Conquer

Willis Hall
The Long and the Short and the Tall

Thomas Hardy
Far from the Madding Crowd

Thomas Hardy
The Mayor of Casterbridge

Thomas Hardy
Tess of the d'Urbervilles

Thomas Hardy
The Withered Arm and other Wessex Tales

L.P. Hartley
The Go-Between

Seamus Heaney
Selected Poems

Susan Hill
I'm the King of the Castle

Barry Hines
A Kestrel for a Knave

Louise Lawrence
Children of the Dust

Harper Lee
To Kill a Mockingbird

Laurie Lee
Cider with Rosie

Arthur Miller
The Crucible

Arthur Miller
A View from the Bridge

Robert O'Brien
Z for Zachariah

Frank O'Connor
My Oedipus Complex and Other Stories

George Orwell
Animal Farm

J.B. Priestley
An Inspector Calls

J.B. Priestley
When We Are Married

Willy Russell
Educating Rita

Willy Russell
Our Day Out

J.D. Salinger
The Catcher in the Rye

William Shakespeare
Henry IV Part 1

William Shakespeare
Henry V

William Shakespeare
Julius Caesar

William Shakespeare
Macbeth

William Shakespeare
The Merchant of Venice

William Shakespeare
A Midsummer Night's Dream

William Shakespeare
Much Ado About Nothing

William Shakespeare
Romeo and Juliet

William Shakespeare
The Tempest

William Shakespeare
Twelfth Night

George Bernard Shaw
Pygmalion

Mary Shelley
Frankenstein

R.C. Sherriff
Journey's End

Rukshana Smith
Salt on the Snow

John Steinbeck
Of Mice and Men

Robert Louis Stevenson
Dr Jekyll and Mr Hyde

Jonathan Swift
Gulliver's Travels

Robert Swindells
Daz 4 Zoe

Mildred D. Taylor
Roll of Thunder, Hear My Cry

Mark Twain
Huckleberry Finn

James Watson
Talking in Whispers

Edith Wharton
Ethan Frome

William Wordsworth
Selected Poems

A Choice of Poets

Mystery Stories of the Nineteenth Century including The Signalman

Nineteenth Century Short Stories

Poetry of the First World War

Six Women Poets

NOTES

NOTES